MAMMALS OF THE CENTRAL ROCKIES

JAN L. WASSINK

Mountain Press Publishing Company
Missoula, Montana
1993

Cover design by Tim Christensen

Library of Congress Cataloging-in-Publication Data

Wassink, Jan L.
    Mammals of the central Rockies   /   Jan L. Wassink.
       p.   cm.
    Includes bibliographical references and index.
    ISBN 0-87842-237-4 (pbk.) : $12.00
    1. Mammals—Rocky Mountains.   2. Wildlife watching—
Rocky Mountains.   I. Title.
QL719.R63W37   1993
599.09787—dc20   92-46268
                                                   CIP

Printed in Hong Kong by Mantec Production Company

MOUNTAIN PRESS PUBLISHING COMPANY
P.O. Box 2399 • Missoula, Montana 59806
(406) 728-1900 • (800) 234-5308

To my wife,
Dar,
who has smoothed many
rough places.

Contents

Map showing the central Rockies (shaded) and locations of national parks and wildlife refuges.

The Central Rockies

More than 180,000 square miles of mountainous terrain make up the Central Rockies, extending from Yellowstone National Park in Wyoming southward almost to the southern border of Colorado, and from the prairies in the east to the desert country of the Great Basin in the west. The Central Rockies are home to a rich and diverse array of mammals. Nature lovers seeking to glimpse this diversity can roam habitats that range from marshy shores, sagebrush flats, and agricultural cropland in the valleys to expansive montane forests at the mid-elevations, and alpine meadows and mountaintops that exceed 14,000 feet. Fifteen national wildlife refuges, including Seedskadee National Wildlife Refuge in Wyoming and Brown's Park and Alamosa national wildlife refuges in Colorado, have been set aside to protect important habitat for migrating and nesting waterfowl, and are home to numerous mammals. Wilderness areas, national monuments, national recreation areas, and national parks help to maintain the beauty and integrity of the region's wildlife habitats. The United States Forest Service and the Bureau of Land Management administer other wide expanses for multiple use, one of which is wildlife values. There can be little doubt that the Central Rockies provide excellent opportunities for careful observers to enjoy viewing the resident mammals.

Mountain lion —T. Ulrich

Introduction

Large mammals have fascinated me for as long as I can remember. While growing up in Iowa, I was thrilled by even a glimpse of a deer. Smaller mammals were much more common, and as I became more aware of them, I found them almost as fascinating. What is it? soon gave way to What does it eat? How does it survive the winter? Where does it den? Why do I see it only in river bottoms?

This book provides an easy-to-use field guide to many of the common and most often seen mammals of the Central Rockies. Field marks are given to aid in identification. The basic natural history information provides insights into the daily lives of these mammals. I hope that many of the questions you will ask, as your interest in mammals deepens and your knowledge expands, will be answered here.

How to Use This Book

Approximately 125 species of mammals make their home in the Central Rockies, as indicated by the checklists of Rocky Mountain National Park, fifteen national wildlife refuges in Wyoming, Colorado, eastern Idaho and eastern Utah, as well as the *Colorado Mammal Distribution Latilong Study* and R. R. Lechleitner's *Wild Mammals of Colorado* (see Suggested References). All of the large, more visible mammals are included in this book, but only representative species of the smaller varieties are described. Particular species were selected on the basis of abundance, ease of identification, and the likelihood that the casual observer will encounter them. At least one example from each of the families of mammals regularly found in the region has been included.

Nomenclature follows Jones et al. (1986) "Revised Checklist of North American Mammals North of Mexico." I have departed from the convention of following the order of families from the simplest to the more complex. Instead, I chose to begin with the largest and most visible mammals and progressed down to the smaller and less easily seen mammals.

For easy identification, a photo accompanies the description of each mammal. To identify a mammal, simply locate its photo in the book and look nearby to learn its name. You will see two names: a Latin name and a common name. The common name is probably the one you will learn first, but the Latin name is also important, because it will help you recognize relationships between different mammals.

Elk cow and bull —J. L. Wassink

Female mink —J. L. Wassink

Scientists classify mammals, like all living organisms, according to their physical similarities and differences. The seven divisions in this system are—from most general to most specific—kingdom, phylum, class, order, family, genus, and species. The species includes individuals that exhibit virtually identical characteristics and breed with each other when given the opportunity. The genus consists of one or more species that are very similar to each other but do not interbreed. The names of these two groups, the genus and the species, make up the Latin name. In this classification system each species has a unique scientific name. A Russian scientist reading about *Mustela vison* knows that he is reading about the mink found in North America and not the one found in England, Central Europe, and northern Asia, which is known as *Mustela lutreola*.

The **description** section provides the characteristics of the mammal as you will see them in the field. Coloration, size, shape, and special characteristics such as antler shape are all important in identifying a mammal.

Similar species describes other species that may superficially resemble the mammal illustrated and lists their distinguishing characteristics. A glance at the photos illustrating those species should quickly confirm your identification.

The **habitat/distribution** notation relates the general areas of the region where the mammal lives, its relative abundance in those areas, and perhaps some suggestions on where to look for it. Rocky Mountain National Park is abbreviated RMNP.

The main **description** of each mammal defines its "niche"— how, when, and where it feeds, breeds, and attracts mates, and whether its populations are going up or down. Distinctive behavior is also described. General family characteristics are given in the family descriptions and may not be repeated in the individual write-ups, so be sure to check the family descriptions for characteristics common to the whole group.

Observing Mammals

The best time to watch mammals is anytime you can. You will greatly increase your viewing success and enjoyment, however, if you know what time of day certain mammals are active and look for them then. For example, if you want to observe deer, watch for them at dawn or dusk, when they are most active. Likewise, tree squirrels are most vocal and active during the daylight hours, so that is the best time to spy on them.

You may be able to observe mammals from your vehicle by stopping and scanning suitable habitats with binoculars. But it is often more enjoyable to get out, walk slowly and quietly through an area, and use your ears as well as your eyes to locate animals. If you hear something or see a movement, concentrate on that spot until you can pinpoint the source with your binoculars and identify it. Animals will often quiet down and stop moving around when you first walk into an area, and it will seem as if there is not a living creature within miles. Sit down and wait, or stand quietly, and you may soon see various mammals as they resume their normal activities. Unlike birds, which leave little sign of their presence, mammals leave distinctive tracks, droppings, and other signs. From these clues, knowledgeable observers can not only tell that mammals are in the area, but know which species they are.

Attracting Mammals

Mammals live only where they can satisfy their basic requirements for food, water, cover, and den sites. Because they are not as mobile as birds, they are not as easily attracted to places where they can be readily observed. Still, there are some things you can do to increase the likelihood of seeing mammals near your home.

Locate feeders nearby to provide the food portion of the equation. Deer may frequent areas where salt, hay, or suitable pelleted food is provided. Tree squirrels may visit feeders that offer corn. Mice and chipmunks frequent the ground under and around bird feeders to nibble on spilled birdseed. Whatever mammal you try to attract, place the feeder near cover but in a spot easily visible from the house. Mammals may also be attracted by birdbaths, fountains, puddles, or sprinklers. Like the feeders, they should be where you will be able to see any visitors.

Most mammals build their own nests, but those that use tree cavities, such as flying squirrels, may use nest boxes if they are located in appropriate habitat and are of suitable size. Bats too may be attracted by roosting boxes, and the practice of providing these houses is becoming increasingly popular. Plans are available from Bat Conservation International (see Suggested References).

Other appropriate food and cover for mammals can be provided through carefully chosen landscaping. Nut trees or berry bushes may attract squirrels and chipmunks. Other plantings—hedges, shrubs, and trees—may provide cover for rabbits and various other small mammals. Whatever you do to attract mammals, be patient. It may take days, weeks, or even months for mammals to locate

White-tailed deer —J. L. Wassink

these new resources, but once they do, they will stay as long as those resources are available. No matter how small your property is, careful planning can create some suitable habitat. Whether you want to attract a few more mammals to your backyard or turn it into a full-fledged wildlife sanctuary, the National Wildlife Federation sponsors a backyard habitat program that can help you every step of the way.

Mammal Ecology

Mammals do not exist in a vacuum but as an integral part of the ecosystem. The ecosystem functions as a whole, with all parts intertwined and working together. Consequently, altering a single strand of this "web of life" affects the entire system. Floods, fires, earthquakes, drought, diseases, insect plagues, and other natural events all contribute to a constantly changing balance of nature. In addition, human activities—farming, logging, mining, road building, stream channelization, fire suppression, suburban sprawl, air and water pollution—throw even more factors into the equation. As site conditions are altered, the complement of mammals living there also changes.

Scientists have identified broad areas, called *biomes* or *life zones*, that support similar communities of plants and animals. These regions share similar climates, elevations, soil types, and other characteristics. The Central Rockies consists of four life zones: the alpine tundra, the subalpine forest, the montane forest, and the upper Sonoran.

The **alpine tundra** is easily recognized by its lack of trees. Here, on the mountaintops, the bitterly cold winter winds freeze-dry any vegetation not insulated by a blanket of snow, thus preventing its growth. Consequently, few woody plants grow here and the existing vegetation is primarily low-growing perennials. The first trees growing downslope from the alpine tundra are subalpine fir, white pine, and Engelmann spruce. These form the **subalpine forest**. The **montane forest**, still lower in elevation, supports Douglas fir, ponderosa pine, quaking aspen, and blue spruce. The **upper Sonoran** life zone, the driest in the region, supports mostly sagebrush, piñon, and juniper.

Plant and animal species form a continuum through the life zones. Some mammals, such as coyotes, have broad environmental requirements, and you may see them anywhere in the region in any of the four life zones. Other mammals may find their requirements are met in very restricted areas of a single life zone. Knowing a mammal's habitat restrictions can help you identify unfamiliar species. The meadow vole, for example, lives primarily in grassy habitats. When you see a volelike mammal in timbered habitat, you can be pretty sure it is not a meadow vole.

Within a life zone, each species of mammal has its own particular way of living—it feeds, dens, moves, and mates in its own unique fashion. Otters spend much of their time in water and feed mainly on fish. A smaller relative, the mink, although an excellent swimmer, stays close to the shoreline, where it feeds in shallow water on small fish, frogs, crayfish, and other similar prey. Nearby, in moist habitats but on the land side of the shoreline, long-tailed weasels live and feed on mice and other small creatures. Still drier habitats are home to the ermine, and upland, timbered habitats provide hunting grounds for pine martens, which are excellent tree climbers. These individual ways of living are called ecological *niches*. The description for each mammal in this book includes information on its special niche.

Territoriality

All wildlife must compete to some degree with others of their species for food, water, cover, and the right to reproduce. Excessive fighting over these resources uses up valuable energy and may

Short-tailed weasel with deer mouse —J. L. Wassink

leave animals weak or crippled. Each species has behavior patterns that allow the distribution of those resources to the fittest individuals with a minimum of fighting.

One way fighting is minimized is through territorial behavior, or land ownership. Some species of mammals claim territories that they defend by marking with urine or scents from special glands. Transient mammals encountering these scent posts are instantly aware that they are entering an occupied territory. If possible, the intruder will avoid the resident mammal. A resident mammal has a definite psychological advantage over an intruder, who usually gives way without a fight. In an actual fight, which is rare, the residents are seldom defeated.

Prairie dogs defend their territories as family groups. They are social animals and live in large "towns" of up to one thousand individuals. These towns may be divided into wards by streams, ridges, gullies, and other natural boundaries. The wards, in turn, are divided into coteries, which are the real social unit of the population.

Although the members of the coterie constantly change through birth, death, and emigration, the territorial boundaries remain the same. They are established, maintained, and passed on to the

Black-tailed prairie dogs —J. L. Wassink

young through constant social contact. A steady pattern of acceptance and mutual grooming by coterie members, and rejection by territorial neighbors, teaches the young the location of boundaries.

Most of the other mammals in the Central Rockies do not actively defend territories. Instead, they live in a home range, which is simply the area where an animal spends its time.

However, even those mammals have methods of sharing resources, with the best going to the fittest. Large carnivores, like the cougar, practice what could be called mutual avoidance. Even though the home ranges of adjacent cougars may overlap to some degree, the animals themselves rarely meet. During their daily travels, cougars mark the boundaries of their range and prominent features within it by urine sprinkling. Another cougar, coming across one of these fresh scents, will avoid contact with the "resident" cougar.

This pattern of passive defense of home ranges is broken by a female cougar with kittens. Highly territorial for a time, she will vigorously defend the area immediately around the den against all other cougars.

As with most animals, the most aggressive and fittest occupy the best home ranges and so have the best chance to survive to reproduce.

Mountain goat kid —J. L. Wassink

Mammal-Watching Ethics

Life is tenuous at best for wild mammals, as they occupy themselves finding food, defending territories, raising young, migrating, escaping predators, and seeking shelter from the weather. In our desire to learn more about them and enjoy them, we need to use some common sense to avoid disrupting their lives to the extent that we threaten their survival.

Mammals are individuals and have different levels of tolerance. Large mammals in refuges and other protected areas are generally more accustomed to people and are more tolerant than they would be in other areas. Small mammals are generally more tolerant than larger mammals but that is not always the case. Many mammals will disappear at the slightest disturbance of their routine, while others may go about their business as usual whether you are there or not.

Den sites are particularly susceptible to disruptions. Some mammals will move their young to another den when disturbed. So, if you find a den, watch it from a distance. Your presence may keep the adults away from the den without you realizing it. If they stay away too long, the young may be stressed by not getting milk when they need it. They may even die—without your knowledge that anything was amiss.

Watching mammals is most enjoyable when they can be observed going about their normal activities. Mammals that do not mind your presence will look in your direction at first but then will settle down and virtually ignore you. If they repeatedly look in your direction, turn away from you, or walk away, you are too close. Retreat, or leave if you have to, until the animals calm down. Handling young animals or altering vegetation around a den may increase the likelihood of predation by drawing attention to the site

Mountain goats and observer —J. L. Wassink

Pronghorn and photographer —J. L. Wassink

by scent or by exposing it to view. Repeatedly spooking animals from favored feeding areas can force them to remain in areas with less food and effectively deprive them of needed energy.

Observing wildlife is an enjoyable activity and, with care, can be carried on with no harmful effects to the animals. Let's make sure we do not destroy the very thing we are seeking to enjoy.

Welcome to the wonderful world of mammals!

Characteristics of Mammals

Mammals are a diverse group of animals, varying widely in size, shape, and habit. From the fishlike blue whale, which may measure 113 feet in length and weigh 170 tons, to the birdlike bats to the more conventional-looking pygmy shrew, which may measure only 3 inches in length and weigh no more than a dime, they are all ideally suited to their respective habitats.

Mammal is derived from the Latin word *mamma,* which means breast or nipple. All mammals have at least one pair of nipples, and the young are nourished by milk produced by the female. Internally, they have a secondary palate that separates the nasal cavity from the mouth, which allows breathing to occur simultaneously with chewing and suckling.

A more easily observed characteristic of mammals is the presence of hair. Hair or fur functions both as insulation and as protection. In small mammals, fur thickness and size are correlated, while for mammals the size of a fox or larger, there is no clear correlation between fur thickness and body size. Apparently, in the larger mammals insulation has reached a useful maximum, whereas in the small forms the fur must be short and light enough for the animals to move about easily.

Like birds, mammals are capable of maintaining their body at a relatively constant temperature. With the fewer hours of daylight in fall, mammals begin growing a coat of fur that is longer than their summer coat and more effective protection against winter temperatures. If insulation alone is not sufficient protection, internal mechanisms trigger shivering, which works the muscles and generates metabolic heat. On the other hand, to combat excessive summer heat, mammals shed some of their hair, pant, sweat, rest in cool dens or dense groves of trees, and move about only in the cooler times of the day.

More than any other group, mammals are aware of what goes on around them. They have highly developed nervous systems and their senses of smell, sight, touch, and hearing are very sensitive.

Order Artiodactyla
Even-toed Ungulates

The three families of Artiodactyls in the Central Rockies are easily distinguished from each other and from other large mammals by the presence and characteristics of horns or antlers. The family Cervidae is the deer family and includes the elk, white-tailed deer, mule deer, and moose. The males of this family have antlers that are shed each year. Both male and female mountain sheep, bison, and mountain goats, family Bovidae, have horns that grow continually and are never shed. Both sexes of pronghorn, the only member of the family Antilocapridae, also have horns, although those of the male are much larger. The outer sheath of pronghorn horns is shed each year.

As a group, the Artiodactyls seem to be assigned the role of converting plant material into animal matter and providing food for the large predators. Their protection against the flesh eaters consists mainly in fleetness of foot, keen hearing, and a wide range of vision, as evidenced by the large eyes set in the sides of the head. They are poorly equipped to actively resist attack by the larger carnivores, and their best defense is flight.

Cloven-hoofed cud chewers, they are specialized for fast, easy travel to escape predators, negotiate rough terrain in search of food, and migrate in response to floods, drought, fires, and seasonal variations in weather. Their speed and ease of movement result from their body being supported on the tips of the third and fourth toes, giving them additional leverage when walking or running.

They are both browsers (eat twigs of trees and shrubs) and grazers (eat forbs and grasses). They have lower incisors but no upper incisors, which forces them to eat by breaking off plants rather than cutting them. Ungulates have strong molars with broad grinding surfaces to mechanically break down the plant food they live on, and four-chambered stomachs, allowing efficient digestion of plant fibers.

Doe and buck pronghorn —J. L. Wassink

Mountain goat taking a dirt bath —J. L. Wassink
Buck mule deer —J. L. Wassink

Horns and Antlers

True horns are found only on mountain goats, mountain sheep, and bison. Horns are never branched but may be curved. Both males and females have horns but those of the females are usually smaller.

Horns originate from a hollow bony core formed by the frontal bone of the skull. Around this core is a hard sheath made of *keratin* (the same substance as our fingernails). Since horns grow continuously from their base, older animals, given equivalent diet, heredity, etc., will have larger horns. Horns grow at varying rates during different seasons of the year. In winter they grow very slowly, forming a deep groove around the base of the horn. In summer they grow more rapidly, forming a fairly smooth area. An animal's age can be determined by counting the number of prominent grooves on the horns (the first ring is formed at one and a half years). As the animal gets older, the horns grow more slowly and the grooves tend to run together, making it more difficult to determine age accurately.

Members of the deer family—elk, moose, and deer—have antlers. Bony prominences (called *pedicels*) located on the frontal bone of the skull form the base for these amazing structures, which are composed of solid bone. Antlers are usually branched except on young or very old animals, which may have single spikes. Normally, only the males have antlers, but occasionally a female with antlers will be seen. Unlike horns, antlers are shed each year.

In early spring, triggered by the increasing photoperiod, antler growth begins. At first, the only evidence is a slight swelling over the pedicel. These swellings soon grow into knobs, then into large, bulbous growths, and finally into recognizable antlers. The developing antlers are covered with a fuzzy skin called *velvet*. Blood in the velvet supplies the antlers with the nutrients necessary for their rapid growth, which may be as much as half an inch a day. Because the growing antlers consist of soft, spongy bone and the blood vessels are near the surface in the velvet, the antlers are very delicate and bleed readily. Bulls and bucks are particularly careful during summer to avoid damaging their antlers on trees. The blood running under the velvet makes the growing antlers feel hot to the touch and may help cool the animals on hot summer days.

By the end of summer, the antlers are full-grown and the blood stops flowing. Rising levels of testosterone, a male hormone that

Crooked horned bighorn sheep ewe —J. L. Wassink

Bighorn sheep showing chips in horns from butting heads —J. L. Wassink

Bull bison —J. L. Wassink

Mountain goat —J. L. Wassink

causes antlers to harden, also cause bucks to become aggressive, and some of the tension is taken out on young saplings. The velvet, which dries during the early stages of the aggressive period, is knocked off during the brush busting—a process that may take less than twenty-four hours. The rubbing continues throughout the breeding season, giving the antler points a high polish. The brownish stain on the remainder of the antler is discoloration from dried blood, not stain from bark.

Bucks and bulls with large racks are generally more successful in finding and breeding females. Active breeding maintains the level of testosterone in the animal's system and postpones the shedding process, which takes place between late November and March.

After being shed, antlers take on a new function. Because of their high content of salts, calcium, phosphorous, and other minerals, they provide a ready source of minerals for mice, chipmunks, porcupines, squirrels, and other rodents. Antlers that drop off in wet areas and are not discovered by one of the small rodents decompose rapidly. Those shed in drier areas last a little longer, but eventually they too decompose and return their nutrients to the soil.

Pronghorns have neither true horns nor antlers. Pronghorn horns resemble true horns in the way they grow and antlers because they are shed every year. Consisting of a keratin sheath growing over a bony core, pronghorn horns grow from the tip of the bony core, while true horns grow from the base. Both sexes have horns, although those of the female are much smaller. Also, unlike true horns, pronghorn horns are branched and have a prong located somewhere opposite the tip of the core.

The new growth starts about September 1. By mid-October, the new growth has loosened the old sheath enough to cause it to drop off, usually sometime in November. Much softer than antlers, pronghorn horns decompose more rapidly than antlers and are seldom found, even by observant naturalists.

Bull elk —J. L. Wassink

Bull elk in velvet —J. L. Wassink

Mule deer buck in velvet —J.L.Wassink

Pronghorn buck —J. L. Wassink

Elk

Description: Brown to yellowish brown body; darker brown on head, neck, and legs; yellowish to orangish rump patch; hair on neck and mane much longer in bulls than in cows. Bulls, 4 to 5 feet high at the shoulder; 600 to 1,000 pounds; antlers from 12-inch single spike to seven-point antlers 48 inches high. Cows, 500 to 600 pounds; no antlers.

Similar species: Mule deer—smaller, black on tip of tail.

Habitat/Distribution: Found in coniferous forests with grassy clearings (meadows, grasslands, burns, and logged areas) throughout the region and in RMNP. Intolerant of human disturbance and overhunting.

Food: Grasses, sedges, forbs, shrubs (willow, serviceberry, snowbrush, sagebrush, etc.), and trees (chokecherry, maple, fir).

Elk usually feed actively from the predawn darkness to about midmorning, when they rest and chew their cud. They may feed sporadically during the day but often do not move much until midafternoon, when they begin feeding again. They often bed high on mountain slopes, where they have a good view of the surrounding area and rising thermals bring the scent of other forest inhabitants from below. In bad weather, they seek more sheltered sites for protection from the elements.

Elk are gregarious and remain in herds throughout the year. Summer herds, consisting of cows, calves, and young (spike) bulls— usually led by an old cow—are often found above timberline or in grassy clearings just below timberline. Mature bulls spend the summer off by themselves in groups of up to three or four.

The normally calm summer routine of feeding and resting throughout the day is suddenly disrupted in September when the rut begins. Bulls begin thrashing bushes and small trees in late August and early September to relieve tensions caused by increasing levels of testosterone. They begin bugling to broadcast their presence to other bulls, and the larger bulls join one of the cow herds and assume the responsibility of keeping other bulls away. When a cow comes into heat, the bull stays close to her until she is bred and then leaves to attend another cow that is in heat. Cows are capable of breeding at two and a half years.

Bull elk —J. L. Wassink

Herd bulls often run themselves ragged in their attempts to keep the cows together and other bulls away. After the breeding season, thinner and exhausted, the bulls wander off by themselves and attempt to put on enough fat to survive the coming winter. The cow herds, left to themselves once again, begin moving down to exposed southern slopes at lower elevations when deepening snow piles up to about 20 inches.

In spring, sometime in late May or early June, the expectant cow separates herself from the rest of the herd and seeks out a secluded spot to give birth to her thirty-to-forty-pound youngster. Usually a single calf is born, but twins are not unheard of. The calf can walk within hours. Within a week, as soon as the calf is capable of keeping up, the pair return to the companionship and protection of the herd.

Once with the herd, the young calf learns quickly. Spurred on by curiosity, it begins sampling green vegetation and learns which plants are good to eat. By playing and cavorting with the other calves, it learns to act like an elk and establishes its rank within the herd. By growing up together, the youngsters develop a social order that stays with them into adulthood. With this social structure in place, fighting is minimized and the herd lives in relative tranquillity.

Calving success varies dramatically in relation to the severity of the winter and habitat conditions. If critical forage is nonexistent or covered by unusually deep snow, the cows may abort. Or, if carried to term, the calf may be underweight and less likely to survive than those with mothers who were better nourished during pregnancy. Because of this nutritional bottleneck, elk are very sensitive to disturbance. Human activities that decrease the quantity or quality of elk winter range have a significant influence on elk populations. The goal of elk management is to keep elk populations in balance with their winter range. Hopefully, this goal will be reached in the future by protecting and improving winter ranges and not by reducing numbers of elk.

Bull elk —J. L. Wassink

Cow elk —J. L. Wassink

Elk calf —T. J. Ulrich

Mule Deer

Odocoileus hemionus

Description: Gray in winter, brown in summer; dark forehead and brisket; white chin, throat, and rump; short, round tail with a black tip; large ears; antlers fork and then fork again. Bucks, 3 to 3½ feet high at the shoulder; 250 to 400 pounds. Does, 120 to 180 pounds; no antlers.

Similar species: White-tailed deer—antler tines all rise off the main beam; tail is large and flat; no rump patch.

Habitat/Distribution: Found throughout the region and in RMNP in brushy coulees, breaks in the desert, and grasslands to above timberline. It also occupies riparian habitats, open to dense montane to subalpine coniferous or aspen forest. It is numerous and has adapted well to people, venturing down into suburban backyards to feed on ornamental shrubs, fruit trees, and a variety of garden plants.

Food: Browse on serviceberry, bitterbrush, mountain mahogany, chokecherry, sagebrush, grasses, and forbs.

Exactly where you will find mule deer depends on the season. They spend the summers on high mountain pastures—alpine meadows, recent burns, or logged areas. As winter comes and snow depths reach 14 inches, mule deer migrate, sometimes over long distances, to their winter range. There, on lower south-facing slopes and other areas where movement is not limited by snow depths and browse is plentiful, they pass the winter.

Gregarious and crepuscular, small groups of mule deer move around and feed early and late in the day. When spooked, they usually run uphill and try to put a hill between them and the source of the disturbance. Occasionally, when running away from an intruder, they may bounce with all four feet working together, looking strangely like a four-legged pogo stick. Frequently, they will pause at the crest of the hill for one last look before disappearing over the hill.

As November approaches, bucks become increasingly active, their necks swell, and they become intolerant of each other. Posturing is usually enough to discourage smaller bucks from coming too close, but bucks of similar size, competing for a receptive doe, may engage in prolonged shoving matches. Actual fighting is not as common as with white-tailed deer.

Mule deer buck —J. L. Wassink

Bucks are moving with the does by mid-November. When he discovers a doe in estrus, the buck accompanies her and keeps other bucks away until she is no longer receptive. He then goes off in search of another whirlwind romance. Because the dominant buck cannot attend two does at the same time, subordinate bucks may get a chance to pass on their genes when several does come into estrus simultaneously.

By mid-December, things have settled down. Does and fawns usually go into the winter in good shape. Bucks, on the other hand, may be thin and exhausted from tending does and chasing other bucks. By January, the bucks have lost their antlers and blend in with the herds of does and fawns.

Fawns are born in late May or June. First-time mothers, usually yearlings, normally have a single spotted fawn. After the first year, the doe will usually have twin fawns if enough food is available.

Hiders rather than followers, the fawns remain behind while the doe goes off to feed. Spotted coats help them blend into the surrounding vegetation, and their almost total lack of scent makes it difficult for predators, such as coyotes and bobcats, to locate them. Six to 10 pounds at birth, they grow rapidly. Within two weeks the fawns are able to keep up with the doe and follow her everywhere. Weaning takes place at about six weeks, although the fawns may try to nurse well into the fall. Young does may stay with their mothers for two years but young bucks may leave the following spring.

Mule deer have excellent eyesight but depend heavily upon their sense of hearing to detect danger, and their strong legs to carry them out of harm's way. Effective against predators and hunters, these senses are no match for the biggest killer of mule deer— winter. Even in mild winters, up to 20 percent of the population, particularly fawns, yearlings, and bucks stressed by the rut, will not live until spring. In harsh winters, mortality may take 70 percent of the population. Like elk, the future of mule deer depends on our ability to preserve their historic winter ranges. Habitats filled with houses and shopping centers and covered with asphalt cannot support many mule deer.

Mule deer bucks —W. Shattil & R. Rozinski

Mule deer does —J. L. Wassink
Mule deer fawn —T. J. Ulrich

White-tailed Deer *Odocoileus virginianus*

Description: Winter, grayish brown; summer, reddish brown; slim, sleek, graceful appearance; foot-long tail white below and brown above; small ears; tines on antlers all rise from a single main beam and do not fork. Bucks, 3 to 3½ feet high at the shoulder; 250 to 350 pounds. Does, 120 to 180 pounds; no antlers.

Similar species: Mule deer—has rump patch; black tip on tail; antlers fork and fork again.

Habitat/Distribution: The white-tailed deer prefers more dense habitats than the mule deer, but it may also be found in grasslands with hardly any tree cover. Very adaptable, it often lives near dense population centers and fares very well in agricultural areas. Although it will probably never be as numerous in this region as the mule deer, its numbers along river bottoms and in dense woodlands in parts of the region continue to grow. Still absent from most of western Colorado, eastern Utah, and RMNP.

Food: Very adaptable; browses on a wide variety of shrubs (choke-cherry, serviceberry, snowberry, and dogwood); also eats apples, alfalfa, corn, peas, lettuce, and sweet corn from gardens.

At first glance, the whitetail does not appear to be anything special. Compared to the other members of the deer family found in the region—mule deer, elk, and moose—the whitetail looks small and delicate. Its streamlined shape, slick coat, and graceful bearing seem to contradict its status as the most abundant and widespread member of the deer family in North America.

The whitetail has several characteristics that allow it to adapt to human environments while other animals simply disappear. The most furtive and elusive of the deer family, it is a nervous, high-strung creature. Where it is hunted, it is as formless and shifty as a wisp of woodsmoke. But where it is protected, as in national parks and hunting preserves, the whitetail is bold and obvious.

Nocturnal and secretive, white-tailed deer may be common in areas where they are rarely seen. Like mule deer, they are most often seen in early morning or late evening. When disturbed, they raise their white tails, which alerts nearby deer that something is amiss. They run smoothly and may occasionally take a high bound.

Most of their lives are spent on relatively small home ranges. Within that range, they habitually use the same trails, feeding

White-tailed deer buck —J. L. Wassink

areas, and bedding areas. Winter may force them to move short distances but usually not very far. Although they are mostly solitary, they are fairly tolerant of one another and often feed side by side.

During the rut, white-tailed bucks establish a series of scrapes. They paw at the ground, creating shallow, oblong depressions from 1 to 4 feet long. Scrapes are believed to help the bucks locate receptive does. Bucks follow a regular route of checking scrapes for the scent of a doe in estrus. If one has visited, the buck trails her and stays with her until she is no longer receptive. Breeding biology is quite similar to that of the mule deer. Very prolific, a herd of white-tailed deer living in ideal conditions can double its numbers in less than two years.

Still, as adaptable as the whitetail is, it cannot live without appropriate habitat. It cannot live in shopping centers, browse on highways, or coexist with power mowers and kids playing football. And it cannot live with overpopulation of its own numbers. As is the case with most wildlife, winter is the critical time of the year, and the availability of good winter range is the critical factor in white-tailed deer population levels.

From Michigan monsters that may weigh up to 425 pounds to 50-pound Key deer in southern Florida and the slightly larger Coues deer of Arizona and Mexico, the whitetail is found in virtually all habitats in the lower forty-eight states. Only the dry habitats of the Great Basin and similar habitats farther west to the California coast still lack white-tailed deer.

The white-tailed deer will probably continue to expand its populations into more foothills, up river valleys, and on into the habitats of the western mountains where they are not currently found. This expansion should take place as a result of hunting regulations structured for their benefit; logging, agriculture, and other habitat modification that provides the "edge" needed by whitetails; and the psychological make-up of the animal itself.

White-tailed deer buck —T. J. Ulrich

White-tailed deer doe —J. L. Wassink
White-tailed deer fawn —J. L. Wassink

Moose

Alces alces

Description: Dark brown to black; large, broad, overhanging snout; pendant dewlap (bell) under throat; antlers massive and flat; tail short. Bulls, 5½ to 6 feet high at the shoulder; 800 to 1,200 pounds. Cows, 600 to 800 pounds; no antlers; no dewlap.

Similar species: Elk—pale yellow rump patch.

Habitat/Distribution: Previously found only in the northern part of the region, moose were introduced into Colorado beginning in 1978 and can now be seen in several areas of Colorado, including RMNP. They can be seen in mountain meadows, river valleys, swampy areas, and clear-cuts in summer, and near willow flats or in mature coniferous forests in winter.

Food: Browse on shrubs and small saplings (willows, aspen); aquatic vegetation (they may submerge for three or four minutes at a time). An adult bull may consume 50 to 60 pounds of forage each day. The name "moose" is a mispronunciation of an Algonquin Indian word, *mong-soa,* which means "twig eater."

At first glance, the moose looks like it was designed by a committee—its legs are too long, its neck too short, its body too big, its eyes too small. And its muzzle? Indescribable! Get to know the moose, though, and you will learn to appreciate an animal that is truly in tune with its environment.

The northern coniferous forest, which the moose calls home, is criss-crossed with rivers and streams to swim, bogs to wade, deadfall to step over, and winter snows to negotiate—perfect for "too long" legs. The "too short" neck, although it forces the moose to kneel when grazing, is perfect for reaching up to feed on twigs, which make up 90 percent of its diet.

The high mountains are cool most of the year and downright cold for several months. The "too big" body of the moose has a low ratio of surface area to volume, making it very efficient at conserving heat. Its large size also eliminates all potential predators except grizzly bears and wolves, neither of which is common.

A forest dweller, the moose could not see danger very far away even if it had the eyes of an eagle. Instead, it depends on its nose and its ears. Breezes carry to the moose's nose all information it needs to know about who is out and about in the forest. In addition,

Bull moose —J. L. Wassink

anything moving through the maze of deadfall, fallen branches, and thickets sends an audible warning.

The indescribable muzzle? Perfect for the task of browsing on twigs and stripping the leaves from succulent branches. It also proves useful for feeding on aquatic plants. Lump all these "wrong" parts together and you have an animal perfectly suited to its environment.

Because they follow their mothers soon after birth, moose calves have no need for spots. Russet-brown with a dark stripe down their backs, moose calves weigh 25 to 30 pounds at birth. But on their diet of protein-rich milk, they may gain 150 pounds within the next five months. Most calves are born singly, although twins are relatively common. Triplets are rare. Cow moose are extremely protective of their calves and when surprised or approached too closely become one of the most unpredictable and dangerous of the large ungulates.

By its first winter, the young bull wears small "buttons"—forerunners of the massive antlers of the mature bull. By the following spring, the cow no longer tolerates it and chases it away. The young bull then assumes the primarily solitary lifestyle of an adult moose, associating with other moose only loosely on good feeding grounds and with cows during the breeding season.

Around the beginning of September, bull moose begin cleaning and polishing their antlers in preparation for the rut. Where populations are low, both sexes may travel extensively in search of mates; in areas with good populations, they may form breeding groups and the bulls may fight for the cows. Not as violent as that of elk or deer, the rut may pass quietly with little more than an occasional shoving match. A bull associates with a cow for the few days she is receptive and then moves on. Cows breed at two and a half years, but on good range they may breed as yearlings.

Winter is tough for all large herbivores, and moose are no exception. While energy requirements are highest in cold weather, the quantity and nutritional quality of food is at its lowest. Because its legs are too long, its body too big, its eyes too small, and its muzzle indescribable, the moose is doing well here and should be with us for a long time.

Bull moose —J. L. Wassink

Cow moose —J. L. Wassink
Cow and calf moose —T. J. Ulrich

Pronghorn

Description: Russet-tan on neck, upper sides, back, and legs; white on lower sides, underneath, on rump and two bands across throat; black markings (more pronounced on bucks) on head and side of throat. Bucks, 2½ to 3 feet high at the shoulder; 110 to 130 pounds; black horns with a single forward-pointing prong. Does, 75 to 110 pounds; short horns (1 to 3 inches).

Similar species: Mule deer—no white on sides, black tail. White-tailed deer—no white on sides; no rump patch.

Habitat/Distribution: Common and highly visible in open, rolling sagebrush or grasslands throughout the region; not found in RMNP. Populations were reduced to less than 25,000 in all of North America in 1925, but under good management, they now number more than one-half million.

Food: Spring and summer—forbs and grasses; winter—sagebrush and other shrubs.

With large eyes capable of detecting movement from several miles away and strong, slim legs capable of carrying them cross-country faster than any other North American mammal, the pronghorn is perfectly designed for the prairies and plains. If danger is spotted, a pronghorn snorts and erects the white hairs on its rump, which creates a flash of white believed to warn other pronghorn of danger. If the intrusion persists, strong legs carry them out of reach. They are capable of running at speeds up to 84 miles per hour, but 40 to 50 miles per hour is more common.

Adult bucks establish territories in March and hold them through the September breeding season. Throughout the spring and summer, nonterritorial bucks gather into bachelor herds, while the does and fawns drift on and off the territories. By late September, the territorial bucks try to hold groups of does and fawns on their territories for breeding, and keep other bucks away. Most does breed when one and a half years old, but some may breed as fawns.

After the breeding season, the territories are abandoned, horns are shed, and all ages and both sexes congregate on winter range. During severe winters, herds may drift for long distances in search of food. Fences and other barriers that restrict these movements may limit populations.

Pronghorn buck —J. L. Wassink

Fawning begins in late May. Shortly before giving birth, the doe seeks out a secluded spot, perhaps a shallow depression in which she can escape detection by predators. The doe gets more nervous as the time approaches, standing up, lying down, standing up again. The actual birth may occur while she is either standing or lying down. About 60 percent of first pregnancies result in twins, and almost all subsequent births result in twins.

Immediately after giving birth, the doe carefully grooms the fawn by licking it meticulously from head to hoof—a process that helps establish the maternal bond between the doe and fawn. The fawn soon battles its way to its feet and within an hour has located its mother's udder and is nursing.

After nursing, the fawn wanders off, selects a bed and lies down. The doe moves away to graze and rest. For the next few days, the fawn spends between 20 and 22 hours a day by itself—sleeping.

During these first few days, the fawn is unable to defend itself or outdistance predators. Still, it is not totally at the mercy of its enemies. Its drab coloration blends well with the soil and the prairie plant life, making it difficult to see. Its instinctive reaction to freeze at any unusual sight, sound, or scent also helps it escape detection. In addition, fawns seem to have little or no odor for their first few days of life. Hunting dogs have walked within inches of motionless fawns without discovering them.

For the first weeks, the doe feeds the fawn three or four times a day. Each feeding session consists of several short nursing periods of from one-half to one minute each. As the fawn matures, the doe ends the nursing sessions while the fawn is still hungry, encouraging it to sample plant food, which will soon be the mainstay of its diet.

The fawn rapidly develops its ability to run. The first day or two, it is still shaky and awkward but can run remarkably fast. By the third day it can outrun a man, and after a week it can run smoothly and effortlessly for short distances. Within a couple of weeks, the fawn can keep up with its mother and the two of them join the main herd of does and fawns.

Pronghorn buck showing flared rump patch —J. L. Wassink

Pronghorn doe and twin fawns   J. L. Wassink

Pronghorn herd —J. L. Wassink

Bison

Description: Dark brown overall; massive head with heavy, black, sharply curved horns (both sexes); heavy beard from lower jaw; heavy growth of woolly hair covers the head and forequarters; large hump over shoulder. Bulls, 5 to 6 feet high at the shoulder; up to 2,200 pounds. Cows, 800 to 1,000 pounds.

Similar species: none.

Habitat/Distribution: Formerly inhabited grasslands throughout the region. Today found only in parks, refuges, and game farms; not found in RMNP.

Food: Grasses, sedges, forbs, and some shrubs.

Herd animals, bison are usually found together. Groups of ten to twelve animals, consisting of cows, calves, and young bulls appear to be the basic unit, but several of these groups may forage together to form large herds. Lone animals are usually old bulls that have left the herds.

The rut, which occurs in August, stirs up a lot of activity, as the bulls try to establish or maintain their dominance over rival bulls. Grunting and groaning fill the air as competing bulls push and shove each other with their massive heads in an effort to prove they are stronger than their opponent. If that does not convince one or the other to leave, they may back off about twenty feet and stand facing each other, bellowing and pawing the ground in a last attempt to bluff the other into retreating. Then, simultaneously, they charge. Surprisingly agile for such massive creatures, they reach top speed within a few steps and collide with each other like loaded freight trains. The impact, accompanied by flying dust and debris, would seem to result in crushed skulls, but that is not the case. One or two collisions is usually enough to convince the smaller and lighter of the bulls that enough is enough.

The usually lone calf is born in early spring. Prior to giving birth, the expectant mother wanders off to find a secluded hollow in which to have her calf. Forty pounds at birth, the reddish brown youngster closely resembles the calves of domestic cattle. Within a few days, the calf is strong enough to accompany its mother and the pair return to the main herd. Unpredictable at any time of year, bison

Bull bison —J. L. Wassink

should not be approached too closely for photographs or any other reason.

For centuries, until about 1840, an estimated 60 million bison darkened the Great Plains. The enormous herds moved with the seasons in search of nutritious grasses. They were so numerous that neither the gray wolf nor the Indians, both of whom depended on the bison for food, had any effect on their numbers. Weather, through its inevitable effects on the quantity and quality of grass, was the main factor controlling the numbers of bison—until the coming of the white man.

Before 1840, white men were concerned with exploring and colonizing the new frontier out to the Mississippi River. Then, spurred on by the Mexican War, the California Gold Rush, and the Gadsden Purchase, westward progress proceeded with renewed vigor. Construction of the transcontinental railroad in 1868, which opened vast new territories in the West to settlers, further aided the progress. Divided by the tracks into a southern and a northern herd, the great bison herds became accessible to market hunters.

Easy profits from selling meat, hides, and bones (used as fertilizer) resulted in the killing of millions of bison. Millions more were massacred in an effort to eliminate the Indians' major source of food, shelter, and clothing. Still more bison were destroyed to save the prairie grasses for the great herds of Longhorn cattle that were beginning to move north.

The southern herd had been completely eliminated by 1874. Closed hunting seasons, enacted in Idaho in 1864, in Wyoming in 1871, and in several other states about the same time, slowed the annihilation of the northern herd but did not stop it.

By 1893 only five wild herds still existed. One in Yellowstone National Park was protected. The other four, all in Colorado, were left unprotected. In 1897, the last wild herd outside of Yellowstone, consisting of a bull, two cows, and a calf, was shot in the Lost Park area of South Park.

Today approximately 30,000 bison live on game farms, preserves, and in national parks, the only remnants of the vast herds of bison that once dominated the Great Plains.

Bull bison —J. L. Wassink

Bison cow and calf —J. L. Wassink

Bison herd —J. L. Wassink

Mountain Goat   *Oreamnos americanus*

Description: White; horns and hooves black; tail may have a few black or brown hairs; longer hair under chin may form a beard, especially in winter; pantaloons around the front legs; body compact and chunky; legs short; horns smooth, sharp, curved backward. Billy, 3 to 3½ feet high at the shoulder; 200 to 325 pounds; horns 8 to 10 inches long, sharply curved and strongly tapered from base to tip. Nanny, 150 pounds; horns shorter, thinner, straighter, and less tapered than those of the billy.

Similar species: Mountain sheep—massive, curling horns; not solid white.

Habitat/Distribution: Steep, precipitous terrain. Alpine meadows in summer; steep, windswept, south-facing slopes in winter, sometimes move down into the subalpine forest. Occurred naturally in the region as far south as South Pass in Wyoming. Has since been transplanted to suitable habitat in mountain ranges throughout the region. Very susceptible to disturbance on winter range, and populations have been eliminated from drainages where roads or good trails approach wintering cliffs.

Food: Grasses, sedges, lichens, forbs, and shrubs.

Living atop sharp peaks and knifelike ridges that plummet into wide valleys and deep basins dotted with azure lakes, mountain goats are definitely mammals with a view. Summers on top of the world are short and winters there are typified by blizzards that may rage for days or even weeks. Winds gusting to 100 miles per hour may pile snow 80 feet deep, and temperatures may drop to 50 degrees below zero. One of the few creatures to call this hostile environment home, the mountain goat not only survives here, it thrives.

Several unique physical adaptations allow the mountain goat to move through its steep homeland as easily as we walk across our backyards. The task of following tiny ledges is simplified for them by a body that is flattened from side to side. A skeletal configuration that allows it to draw all four hooves together turns small projections into secure footholds. Short cannon (lower leg) bones and unusually powerful shoulder muscles enable the goat to remain under control as it pulls and picks its way through precipitous terrain. Unusually flexible toes, surfaced with rough, pliable,

Mountain goat billy —J. L. Wassink

convex traction pads and edged by hard horny shell, can either spread wide apart to distribute the animal's grip over a large area, or draw together to hook minute projections.

Protection from the elements is provided by pure white pelage consisting of two layers—the shaggy outer coat of hollow, 8-inch guard hairs and an inner layer of thick, fluffy cashmere-quality wool. The pelage, coupled with the short, thick body that minimizes surface area and therefore heat loss, protects the mountain goat from even the most extreme ridgetop conditions.

Accidents do happen, however, and most mountain goat deaths result from accidents caused by steep slopes, rockslides, icefalls, avalanches, falling snow cornices or ledges, and simple but fatal slips. A number of kids and yearlings, whose smaller bodies put them at a disadvantage in deep snow and extreme temperatures, succumb to extreme weather each year.

Except for mature billies, which are solitary except during the rut, mountain goats are semigregarious and live in small groups of up to five animals. Larger nursery bands of nannies, kids, and immature billies may form during the summer. These bands provide better protection for the kids and allow them to interact with each other and begin to form the social bonds that become important later on.

Mountain goat social interactions are based on a dominance hierarchy. The older, stronger individuals generally dominate the younger, smaller animals by preëmpting pawed feeding craters, sheltered bedsites, salt, and prospective mates. Aggressive adult females dominate all other classes, followed by two-year-old males, two-year-old females, yearlings, and kids. Adult males are effectively subordinate to other classes but not out of fear—when motivated by the presence of salt or during the rut, they may dominate all other classes. In most confrontations, the underdog knows his place and does not really resist. More vigorous battles occur between strangers and goats of similar rank.

Breeding occurs in November and December. Rival billies fight head to tail, sometimes inflicting serious injuries to hindquarters and flanks. Nannies usually breed at two and a half years and have a kid every other year. A single seven-to-eight-pound kid is the norm, with twins occurring once in forty births. Born on an isolated rock outcropping in late May, the kid grows quickly and follows its mother anywhere within a week.

Mountain goat nanny —J. L. Wassink

Bottom of mountain goat foot
—T. J. Ulrich

Mountain goat —T. J. Ulrich

Mountain goat nanny with two kids
—T. J. Ulrich

Bighorn Sheep

Ovis canadensis

Description: Grayish brown with yellowish white underparts; creamy white rump patch around small brown tail. Rams, 3 to 4 feet high at the shoulder; 150 to 350 pounds; horns of adult rams are massive and curled, up to 45 inches long; horns of yearling rams wider at the base with more divergent tips than those of ewes, and 7½ to 17 inches long. Ewes, 150 pounds; horns of adult ewes thin, slightly curved, 6 to 13 inches long.

Similar species: Mountain goat—solid white.

Habitat/Distribution: Cliffs, mountain slopes, rolling foothills, and sometimes intermountain valleys throughout the region and in RMNP.

Food: Summer—wide variety of grasses, sedges, and forbs; winter—bunchgrasses and shrubs.

Two large rams move toward each other with a deliberate, stiff-legged gait, heads extended in a line with their bodies, each with his upper lip curled back in a grimace. As they seem about to pass each other, they stop, each with his head next to the other's shoulder. Several moments pass before either ram moves. One ram moves up to the other, places his head on the other's back, and kicks him with a front leg.

Accepting the challenge, the ram responds by turning and pushing the other ram with his chest. After a little more shoving, the pair seem to tire of the game and move off in opposite directions. Suddenly, the challenger turns, rears on his hind legs, and propels himself toward his opponent. Far from being surprised, the other ram performs the same maneuver almost simultaneously and hurls himself through the air to meet the oncoming living projectile. At the last moment, both rams drop from their hind legs, adding the force of gravity to their forward charge.

Moving at a combined speed of more than 40 miles per hour just before impact, the rams collide with a bone-jarring crash. A resounding *crack* echoes through the canyon as shock waves from the impact ripple back over their muscular bodies, dislodging loose hair and dust. The rams raise their heads, turn them sideways, and stand motionless—each displaying his horns to full advantage and giving his opponent a chance to equate the size of his horns with the force of the blow he has just sustained.

Bighorn sheep ram —J. L. Wassink

These ritualistic battles for dominance occur every November, as bighorn sheep gather on their winter range for the rut. The winner of these battles is usually the ram with the largest horns. He feeds on the choicest forage plants, rests in the most comfortable beds, and controls the willing ewes. After a month or so, the rut ends and the activity in the herd settles down to the winter routine of feeding and resting.

The most sociable of the large ungulates, mountain sheep live in herds segregated according to age and sex. Ewes, lambs, and yearling males band together. Groups of adult males spanning two-or-three-year classes form separate herds.

Around the first of June, just before giving birth, pregnant ewes wander off by themselves to a secluded covert. The lamb (usually one; twins are rare) can follow its mother almost immediately. Within a few days, the mother and lamb rejoin the main herd. This first summer, spent in alpine meadows broken by steep, rugged cliffs, is carefree and filled with playing and cavorting with the other lambs. But the lamb is already beginning to establish its place in the herd.

The social system of the bighorn has an important implication in the management of the species. Bighorns follow age-old migration routes and even use traditional bedding sites on their travels to and from established seasonal ranges. The herd is led by older members, who learned the routes from their elders. In this way, the locations of the ranges are passed from generation to generation.

Before settlers arrived with their domestic livestock, this characteristic was an advantage. But as more and more domestic animals were put on the ranges and the bunchgrasses began to disappear, the bighorns were unable to move on in search of greener pastures. Instead, bound by tradition, they continued to frequent overgrazed ranges and suffered drastic declines from malnutrition and its accompanying diseases.

Reduced competition with domestic livestock, coupled with trap and transplant programs, have allowed some sheep herds to recover. However, in some cases, sheep transplanted onto summer ranges have been unable to locate critical winter ranges and vice versa. Severe winters and diseases carried by domestic sheep appear to be the major limiting factors for mountain sheep populations in the Central Rockies today.

Bighorn sheep rams —J. L. Wassink

Bighorn sheep ewe —J. L. Wassink
Bighorn sheep lamb —J. L. Wassink

Order Carnivora
Carnivores

The order Carnivora includes mammals that are true carnivores and also some that have diverged considerably and are omnivorous (generalized feeders). The main distinguishing characteristic is dentition, which is more or less modified for eating flesh and always includes prominent incisors and canines.

Wolves, coyotes, and foxes (family Canidae) walk on their toes (digitigrade). Their long legs have padded feet with five toes and nonretractile claws. Their teeth are relatively unspecialized, although the lower first molar meshes with the upper fourth premolar to create a shearing action for cutting flesh. The canids capture prey by chasing and kill by slashing with their canines.

Family Ursidae, the bears, have nearly flat-topped molars, much like those of humans, which are adapted more for chewing vegetation than for shearing meat. Bears have flat feet and nonretractile claws, and they walk with all five toes touching the ground (plantigrade).

The family Procyonidae includes what are believed to be the most primitive of the living carnivores. Raccoons and ringtail cats, the only North American members of this family, walk plantigrade and have long tails.

Appropriately named, the family Mustelidae includes a number of mammals that have musk glands at the base of their tails. A varied group, it contains the skunks, badgers, wolverine, and otters, as well as the weasels. Most of the family have long, slim bodies, walk on the tips of their toes, and are very agile. They have short muzzles and extremely sharp teeth that they use to capture and kill prey.

Members of the cat family, Felidae, are highly specialized. They have short, broad skulls, short jaws, and teeth adapted for shearing meat and tendons. Cats are fast runners over short distances and capture prey with a short run from ambush. Since their feet are raised somewhat from the ground, they run on the surfaces of their toes, unlike the hooved mammals, which use the tips.

Coyote —J. L. Wassink

Ermine with deer mouse   J. L. Wassink

Mountain lion showing canines —J. L. Wassink

Coyote

Description: Grayish brown with varying degrees of red on legs, feet, and ears; pointed muzzle; bushy tail; 32 to 40 inches long; 14-inch tail; 30 to 50 pounds.

Similar species: Red fox—reddish in color; holds tail straight when running. Gray fox—smaller; holds tail out straight when running.

Habitat/Distribution: Common throughout the region and in RMNP in open prairies, desert habitats, forests, subalpine and alpine habitats, often found in close proximity to farms, ranches, and suburban areas.

Food: Both carnivores and scavengers—feed on small rodents, grasshoppers, carrion, various fruits and berries; sheep and other domestic livestock are taken on occasion.

Often nicknamed "song dog," coyotes are extremely vocal. Their howling and yipping are commonly heard at dusk and serve as a means of communication. Their vocalizations often betray their presence even where the animals themselves are never seen. Its Latin name, *Canis latrans,* literally means "dog barking."

Creatures of the open, coyotes den up only when they have pups. Although they may seek shelter from the hot sun or heavy rain, their dense coats protect them from everything else.

Coyotes are monogamous and often mate for life. Breeding occurs in February or March. Dens are found or dug under large boulders, in crevices and caves in rocky outcroppings, or in hillsides or banks. The same den may be used from year to year unless the pair is disturbed. From four to seven pups are born in April and progress rapidly from a diet of milk to small mammals. By three to four weeks old, they begin venturing out of the den to play. By eight to nine weeks, they begin following the parents and learn to hunt. At about this time they are weaned and the den is abandoned.

Because coyotes will feed on any plentiful food source, they often take lambs from nearby flocks of domestic sheep. It is no surprise that they are hated and often persecuted by the affected ranchers. In spite of continuing persecution by man and encroaching civilization, coyotes are flourishing. It is my belief that if the earth ever becomes uninhabitable, the coyote will be one of the last mammals to disappear.

Coyote in winter —J. L. Wassink

Coyote —J. L. Wassink

Coyote feeding on elk carcass —J. L. Wassink

Swift Fox

Vulpes velox

Description: Smallest of the canids; buffy yellow color; more grayish above; black tip on tail; white chin, throat, and belly; large ears; 15 to 20 inches long; 10-inch tail; 4 to 6 pounds.

Similar species: Gray fox—larger; black streak on top of tail. Coyote—much larger. Kit fox—larger ears; longer tail; found in dry habitats in the Great Basin.

Habitat/Distribution: Primarily an animal of the Great Plains to the east, inhabits the open desert areas and plains along the eastern edge of the region. Not found in RMNP.

Food: Rodents, especially kangaroo rats; also rabbits, insects, and mice.

Although it was once abundant in parts of the Great Plains, the swift fox was all but eliminated from its range by 1900. Poisons—spread for coyotes and wolves—and trapping decimated its numbers.

Little research has been done on the reproduction of the swift fox. As far as is known, swift fox are monogamous and breeding takes place in January or February. After a two-month gestation, four or five young are born in the underground den. The nesting chamber is located at the end of a burrow 8 to 10 feet long, which angles into the ground at about 45 degrees. The young open their eyes at about twelve days. By one month, they begin emerging from the den. Weaned at six to seven weeks, they resemble the adults at about three months. By five months, they are on their own.

This, the most subterranean of the foxes, is trusting and easily killed. Trapping, shooting, poisoning, and automobiles are the major causes of swift fox mortality. Captive breeding programs are underway to reestablish the swift fox in portions of its historic range.

The similar and closely related kit fox (*Vulpes macrotis*) inhabit the dry, rugged scrublands of the Great Basin. Their large, closely set ears and longer tail distinguish them from the swift fox of the eastern plains. Kit fox feed heavily on black-tailed jackrabbits, cottontails, kangaroo rats, other small mammals, and a variety of other small creatures.

The future of the swift and kit fox depend on our ability to preserve their habitat. Without it, they will not survive.

Swift fox —P. Powell

Swift fox pair —P. Powell
Swift fox showing bushy tail —P. Powell

Red Fox

Vulpes vulpes

Description: Rufous upperparts; white below; typical canine form—pointed ears; slender muzzle; long, bushy rufous tail with white tip; black lower legs and feet; 22 to 25 inches long; 15-inch tail; 7½ to 15 pounds. Female slightly smaller.

Similar species: Coyote, gray fox, swift fox—none are rufous with white-tipped tail.

Habitat/Distribution: The most common and well known of the foxes, and the most widely distributed carnivore in the world because of its ability to use a wide variety of habitats. Open country is a common element in all of them—from agricultural woodlots interspersed with cropland and grass pastureland to alpine tundra. Found in suitable habitats throughout the region and in RMNP.

Food: Primarily voles (often 50 percent of diet); almost anything that is readily available—rabbits, birds, reptiles, amphibians, fruits, berries, insects, eggs, and carrion.

The red fox, and stories about this crafty fellow, have intrigued people for a long time. Its role in folklore can be traced back at least 2,500 years. *Aesop's Fables* have immortalized the fox since 600 B.C. Its well-deserved nickname is "Reynard," from the French *renard,* meaning "unconquerable through his cleverness."

Its reputation as an intelligent animal is enhanced by its appearance. The expressive eyes are bright yellow and, unlike other members of the dog family, have elliptical pupils. An inquisitive nose and upright ears add to the alert look.

Red fox are monogamous and mate for life. Breeding takes place in January or February. The den site, usually a remodeled badger or marmot hole, is prepared in March. By May, after a 51-day gestation, the four to nine pups are born. The vixen stays with the pups for the first nine days, surviving on food brought to the den by the male. For two weeks the young live exclusively on milk. The offerings then expand to include regurgitated food. At about six weeks the young start venturing out of the den. By ten weeks they accompany the adults on hunting forays, and by the end of the summer they are on their own.

The red fox is loved by farmers plagued with an overabundance of mice but hated by farmers with footloose fowl. It is respected by houndsmen and loathed by bird hunters. But every honest observer must admire this intelligent and adaptable animal.

Red fox —J. L. Wassink

Red fox —J. L. Wassink

Red fox pups —J. L. Wassink

Gray Fox

Urocyon cinereoargenteus

Description: Blackish gray above with a dark streak down its spine; reddish below with white throat and belly; black on the muzzle, the tip of the tail, and down the top midline of the tail; short legs; small ears; strongly curved claws; 22 to 30 inches long; 10-to-15-inch tail; 7 to 13 pounds.

Similar species: Coyote—larger, lacks black streak on top of tail. Swift fox—smaller, lacks black streak on top of tail.

Habitat/Distribution: Favors open timber and brushy slopes in the valleys of the region, north to the Wyoming border. Rare in RMNP.

Food: Rabbits, woodrats, mice, voles, squirrels, insects, berries, nuts, and carrion.

Because it prefers heavier cover and is more nocturnal than the red fox, the gray fox is seen less often than its red cousin. And, when disturbed, the gray fox is more likely to slink away into heavy cover than make a mad dash for the nearest hill.

When closely pursued, a gray fox may climb a tree to escape. The only fox that commonly climbs trees, they have often been seen resting or hiding in trees. There are records of them denning and raising young in large, hollow, standing trees, some of which had entrance holes as high as 20 feet off the ground.

More often, dens are located among rocks, in cliffsides, or in hollow trees or logs, and may be reused year after year. Three or four pups are born in April after a two-month gestation period. Born blind and almost hairless, the pups are tended constantly by the mother for three or four days. Food is brought to her by the male. The pups' eyes open at about twelve days but they do not venture out of the den until a month later. After two months of venturing farther and farther from the den, they begin to accompany their parents on hunts. By five months, they go off to establish territories and find mates.

As with most of the canids, their worst enemy is man. Because their pelage is stiff and not soft, like the fur of the other canids, the price of their pelts is low and they are not heavily hunted or trapped for their fur. They are shyer than the red fox and rarely take domestic fowl. In most cases, they are beneficial to man because of the large numbers of mice and voles they eat.

Gray fox —T. J. Ulrich

Gray fox —T. J. Ulrich

Gray fox pups —T. J. Ulrich

Black Bear

Description: Black, brown, or blond hair; long, straight muzzle; slight shoulder hump but highest at the hips; dark, strongly curved front claws less than 1½ inches long; claw marks do not show in tracks. Male, 2 to 3 feet high at the shoulder; 4½ to 5 feet long; 180 to 400 pounds. Female, 120 to 180 pounds.

Similar species: Grizzly bear—larger; dished face; hump on shoulder.

Habitat/Distribution: Fairly common throughout the forested habitats of the region, black bears inhabit dense forests and riparian habitats throughout the year. They generally avoid clear-cuts until the brush and conifers have grown back, except in spring, when they can often be seen on open slopes and in avalanche chutes, searching for fresh green grasses.

Food: Omnivorous in their tastes, they eat grasses, sedges, berries, fruits, the inner bark of trees, insects, honey, eggs, carrion, rodents, ungulates (both wild and domestic), and garbage.

Primarily nocturnal and usually solitary, black bears breed in June or July. After breeding, the females undergo "delayed implantation"—a phenomenon in which the fertilized egg passes into the uterus but changes very little until late fall, when it implants and then begins to grow rapidly. The young, from one to four but usually two, are born naked and blind in the winter den and are fairly well developed before emerging in the spring.

The young stay with the mother until they are almost two years old. The female does not breed the summer after the cubs are born. The cubs may den with her as yearlings. She breeds again the second summer after giving birth and drives the almost-two-year-old cubs out before entering her winter den, where she will give birth to another litter of cubs. The females first breed at either 2½ or 3½ years.

Winter dens are often located in natural cavities found in trees or rocks, or under logs, brush piles, or buildings. The bears line them with leaves, ferns, grasses or similar material. A black bear will occasionally dig a den for itself, but it will be much less elaborate than that of its larger cousin, the grizzly bear.

Black bear —J. L. Wassink

Unlike other carnivores, which remain active, bears sleep away the winter. Preparations for sleep begin early in the fall, when black bears begin feeding with added urgency. In the two or three months before denning, they accumulate enough fat to carry them through the winter and the lean weeks of early spring. When finally ready to enter the den, they have a luxurious coat of three-inch fur and a four-inch layer of fat to keep them warm and well nourished.

Although often referred to as "hibernation," the sleep of bears is not true hibernation. The heart rate, respiration rate, and body temperature of the sleeping bears remain near normal. The bears may occasionally wander out of the den during warm weather, but they do not normally eat, drink, urinate, or defecate during the winter. Their kidneys continue to make urine but it is re-absorbed through the urinary bladder into the bloodstream. Prior to dormancy, bears develop a fecal plug. Although its function is unknown, the plug comes from an accumulation of residual material in the lower colon, closing the alimentary canal. If disturbed, the bears may continue to sleep, not even lifting their heads. They are so lethargic they seem unaware of danger. Awakened in the spring by an internal clock, they venture out in search of tender green grass to restart their systems.

Research is in progress to learn more about the changes bears undergo before, during, and after their winter sleep. Physiologists are studying these animals in the hope of gaining insight into malnutrition and human diseases, such as diabetes. Other scientists believe that understanding the physiology of hibernation and lethargy may revolutionize space travel, suggest new surgical procedures, increase the understanding of the organization of the brain, improve treatment of cancer, or reveal the deep secrets of sleep.

Unlike grizzly bears, black bears climb readily. Their shorter claws provide better leverage and allow them to dig into bark, where the grizzlies' claws would simply slide off. Even very young cubs, when warned of danger by their mother, scamper quickly up nearby trees, often to dizzying heights, until called down by the sow.

Black bear —J. L. Wassink

Black bear cub —T. J. Ulrich

Black bear in winter den —J. L. Wassink

Grizzly Bear

Ursus arctos

Description: Blond, brown, or black, with silver-tipped hair; profile has a dished-in shape; pronounced hump over shoulders; front claws are nearly white, 1½ to 4 inches long, visible in the tracks. Male, 3 to 3½ feet high at the shoulder; 6 to 7 feet long; 300 to 400 pounds but may reach 650 pounds. Female, 200 to 300 pounds.

Similar species: Black bear—smaller; straight face profile; no shoulder hump.

Habitat/Distribution: Rare or extinct in the region except in northern Wyoming and eastern Idaho, where remnant populations are hanging on in the face of habitat encroachment.

Food: Omnivorous: grizzlies eat grasses, roots, bulbs, berries, insects, carrion, fish, rodents, ungulates (young and domestic), and garbage.

More crepuscular than nocturnal, grizzlies are more active early and late in the day than at night. Although they are solitary by nature, they may gather and feed side by side at concentrated food sources.

Like the black bear, they breed in June and July and have their cubs (one to four but usually two) in their winter dens. The young are born blind and naked but develop before emerging from the den. They stay with the female for almost two years and spend their first winter in a den with her. She breeds the second summer after they are born and drives them away before entering her winter den. The young do not breed until they are four to six years old, and thereafter give birth only every two or three years.

Winter dens are excavated on steep, timbered north slopes at high elevations in areas with deep snow cover. The dens are usually dug beneath roots, which support the roof. Grizzlies usually enter their dens during a major snowstorm that covers their tracks and seals the den.

Grizzlies do not climb limbless trees well because of their long claws, but they can and do scramble up trees with limbs that provide them with a purchase.

Incompatible with civilization, grizzlies were poisoned, trapped, and shot into oblivion in Colorado and Utah many years ago. Then, in 1979, a grizzly was killed when it attacked a hunter in the San Juan Mountains in southwestern Colorado. Are there more around? No one knows for sure.

Grizzly bear —T. J. Ulrich

Grizzly sow and cubs —T. J. Ulrich
Grizzly tracks —T. J. Ulrich

Ringtail

Description: Light buff above with black-tipped guard hairs; white or buff-white below; large eyes with white spots above and below; long white tail with black rings and tip. Male, 14 to 16 inches long; 15-inch tail; 1½ to 2½ pounds. Female slightly smaller. Red to yellowish green eyeshine.

Similar species: Raccoon—larger; stockier; tail shorter than body; black mask.

Habitat/Distribution: Fairly common in Colorado, ranging just into the southwest corner of Wyoming. Found in dry habitats from sea level to about 9,200 feet but seldom more than one-quarter mile from a water source.

Food: Omnivorous: the ringtail eats less plant material than raccoons. Insects, small mammals such as woodrats and mice, reptiles, and arthropods are important items in their diet. Fruits, juniper, persimmon, hackberry, acorns, and prickly pear are also eaten.

Although fairly common and active year-round, ringtails are seldom seen and little known because of their nocturnal habits. Strictly nocturnal, they wait until the last hint of light has disappeared before venturing out in search of food. Extremely agile, they run and climb easily but usually catch their prey by ambush.

They den in caves, rock crevices, burrows, brush piles, buildings, and tree hollows, and hollows in tree roots. They accept these hollows as is, making no modifications when they move in. They change dens frequently, sometimes daily.

The breeding season extends from February to June but most of the breeding occurs in March or April. Ringtails are polygamous with no evidence of persistent pair bonds. In May or June, after a gestation of 51 to 54 days, the three or four young are born. Naked, undeveloped, and weighing less than an ounce, they open their ears after 19 to 31 days and their eyes a couple of days later. They continue to develop slowly, and begin foraging with the mother after eight weeks. At about three months, they begin denning separately. Efficient mousers, ringtails are coveted by most people who know them. Totally inoffensive, ringtails are threatened only by habitat loss through urbanization.

Ringtail —R. C. Gildart

Raccoon

Procyon lotor

Description: Hunchbacked appearance; salt-and-pepper color on body; black mask; black-and-white ringed tail. Male, 20 to 26 inches long; 10-inch tail; 20 to 35 pounds. Female slightly smaller.

Similar species: Ringtail—no face mask; slender body; tail longer than body.

Habitat/Distribution: There are believed to be fifteen to twenty times as many raccoons now as in the 1930s. Usually found near water, raccoons inhabit bottomland forests, riparian areas, agricultural lands, and urban areas throughout the region and in RMNP.

Food: Omnivorous—carrion, garbage, birds, mammals, insects, crayfish, mussels, etc.

Contrary to popular belief and in spite of the fact that their Latin name, *lotor,* means "washer," raccoons do not wash their food. However, anyone watching one swish its front paws around in shallow water and then pop a crayfish into its mouth could certainly be fooled into thinking that is what is happening. In reality, the raccoon is merely using its sensitive paws to search for food.

Highly intelligent, raccoons are adaptable and learn quickly. Primarily nocturnal, they may alter their schedule to take advantage of a food source. They can learn to open fasteners to obtain food and can pass these learned abilities on to their young.

Dens are located anywhere that provides shelter—in burrows, hollow trees, piles of rubbish, brush, lumber, corncribs, hay lofts, attics, or chimneys. Breeding occurs in February, and after a 63-day gestation, the young are born in mid-April. Their eyes, closed at birth, open after about 21 days. At nine weeks, they begin moving with the female. By mid-July they are weaned but may remain with the mother through the first winter.

When disturbed, they often climb trees. Raccoons are excellent climbers and can descend trees headfirst. Other times they simply jump, often from great heights, and hit the ground running.

Very adaptable, these interesting mammals can get along very well with civilization unless it includes unregulated hunting and trapping.

Raccoon —T. J. Ulrich

Raccoon searching for food —T. J. Ulrich

Raccoon in winter —T. J. Ulrich

Marten

Description: Mid-brown but varies from almost black to almost orange; pointed face; vertical "eyebrows" above inner corners of eyes; prominent ears; short legs; legs and tail darker than body; head lighter; orange throat or chest patch; long, slender body; long, bushy tail. Male, 14 to 20 inches long; 8-inch tail; 1⅔ to 2¾ pounds. Female, 1½ to 1⅞ pounds.

Similar species: Mink—white on chin; usually found in or near water.

Habitat/Distribution: Fairly common in mixed stands of conifers throughout the higher elevations of the region and in RMNP.

Food: Opportunistic—microtine rodents (voles) in summer; snowshoe hares, ruffed grouse, squirrels, insects, fruits, nuts, berries, and carrion.

Marten are the most arboreal of the weasels, and their semiretractile claws and hindlimbs, which rotate and thus enable them to descend trees headfirst. Although they are very much at home in trees, they spend most of their time on the ground.

Marten hunt when their prey are active. Small prey is killed with a single neck bite; larger prey is wrapped with the legs and body and then killed with a bite. When flying squirrels or snowshoe hares are numerous, they hunt at night. When chipmunks and ground squirrels are more plentiful, they hunt during the day. In winter they are less active than in summer, and during extremely cold weather may time their activities to take place during the warmest part of the day. They may also hunt by tunneling beneath the snow.

Solitary by nature, the males live on a home range of about 1.2 square miles. Females have smaller home ranges—about .4 square miles.

Marten nest in hollow trees or squirrel nests. Induced ovulators and subject to delayed implantation, they breed sometime in late summer, but implantation is delayed until March. Active gestation is about 27 days and two or three young are born in March or April. Weighing only about an ounce at birth, they are blind, almost naked, and helpless. Their ears open at about 24 days and their eyes at 39 days. Weaned at six weeks, they become active outside the den after seven to eight weeks. Even where common, these beautiful mammals are seldom seen. As with most mammals, elimination of their habitat is the major factor affecting their population levels.

Marten —J. L. Wassink

Marten —J. L. Wassink

Marten —J. L. Wassink

Marten —J. L. Wassink

Ermine

Mustela erminea

Description: Summer—dark brown with white underparts and feet. Winter—white except for black tip on tail. Male, 6 to 9 inches long; 2¼-to-4-inch tail; 2½ to 6 ounces. Females, 5 to 7½ inches long; 2-to-3-inch tail; 1 to 3 ounces.

Similar species: Long-tailed weasel—larger; longer tail; no white line connecting the white underparts with the white on the feet in summer. Mink—larger; uniform dark brown year-round.

Habitat/Distribution: Ermine inhabit brushy or wooded areas, usually near water but wherever there is an abundance of mice and voles. There may be as many as twenty weasels per square mile in good habitat and their home ranges vary from about 30 to 40 acres. They occur throughout the region and in RMNP.

Food: Small mammals—mice, voles, chipmunks; small birds, other small creatures.

Ermine, also known as short-tailed weasels and the smallest weasels in the region, are active primarily at night. Like most carnivores, though, they will hunt whenever their prey is active. Their long, thin bodies enable them to follow voles and mice into burrows, cracks, and crevices, a technique the slightly smaller female uses more often than the male. Once the prey is overtaken, the weasels wrap their limber bodies around the animal to hold it. It is then dispatched with a powerful bite at the back of the neck that drives the canine teeth through the base of the skull—a technique characteristic of weasels.

Dens are often located in the burrows of their prey—underground, under stumps, rock piles or buildings. The nest itself is usually lined with mouse fur. The single litter of from four to eight young is born in April or May after an 8½-to-10-month gestation. The young open their eyes between 30 and 45 days. The females mate again soon after giving birth, while still lactating. Young females mate their first summer, sometimes even before their eyes open or they are weaned. The females remain in estrus until they are mated. Because of delayed implantation, the young are not born until the following spring.

Short-tailed weasels are preyed upon by larger carnivores and many birds of prey. In winter, their white coats provide camouflage, and the highly visible black tip on their tail may cause predators, particularly raptors, to strike too far back and thereby miss the body of the weasel.

Ermine, winter coat —J. L. Wassink

Ermine, eclipse coat —J. L. Wassink

Ermine, summer coat —T. J. Ulrich

Long-tailed Weasel   *Mustela frenata*

Description: Summer—yellowish white underparts; brown upper parts; black-tipped tail with no white line down the inside of the hind legs. Winter—solid white except for black tip on tail. Male, 9 to 10½ inches long; 4-to-6-inch tail; 7 to 12 ounces. Female, slightly smaller—8-to-9-inch body; 3-to-5-inch tail; 3 to 7 ounces.

Similar species: Ermine—smaller; tail relatively shorter; white line down inside of leg. Mink—uniform brown color.

Habitat/Distribution: All habitats near water. There may be as many as fifteen to twenty per square mile in good habitat, and the home ranges vary from 30 to 40 acres. They are found in suitable habitats throughout the region and in RMNP.

Food: Generalists—take a wide variety of prey. Males—mice and voles but also snowshoe hares, cottontails, pikas, tree squirrels, ground squirrels, woodrats, prairie dogs, and pocket gophers; some birds. Females—mice and voles but also chipmunks.

Long-tailed weasels are primarily nocturnal but may be active any time of day. Although they hunt mainly on the ground, they are capable of climbing trees in pursuit of tree squirrels, chipmunks, and occasionally, birds. In winter, they may hunt by tunneling under the snow in pursuit of mice and voles. Aboveground, prey is located primarily by scent or sound, subdued by being wrapped up in the weasel's long, lithe body and killed with the single bite to the back of the skull that is characteristic of weasels. Belowground, perhaps due to tight quarters, prey is killed by biting the throat.

The long, slim shape of the weasel, although beneficial while pursuing prey, has a large surface area and loses heat rapidly. Consequently, they have higher metabolic rates than more conventionally shaped mammals and must capture relatively more prey.

Dens are usually obtained by taking over the burrow of its prey, located under wood piles or rock piles. The long-tailed weasel breeds in July or August, but delayed implantation allows the young to be born about nine months later in April or May. The four to eight young open their eyes when about one month old. Breeding biology is similar to the short-tailed weasel, except the females do not come into estrus again until about two months after giving birth and they don't breed for the first time until three or four months old. The males may breed at one year.

Long-tailed weasel —T. J. Ulrich

Long-tailed weasel carrying young —T. J. Ulrich

Young long-tailed weasels —T. J. Ulrich

Mink
Mustela vison

Description: Weasel shape; uniform, rich dark brown color; white chin or throat patch; partially webbed feet. Males, 13 to 17 inches long; 7-to-9-inch tail; 1½ to 3 pounds. Females, 12 to 14 inches long; 5-to-8-inch tail; 1¼ to 2½ pounds. Yellowish green eyeshine.

Similar species: Long-tailed weasel and ermine—smaller with white underparts. Marten—buffy throat and breast. River otter—much larger.

Habitat/Distribution: Usually found near water. Found all across North America except in the Great Basin and the Desert Southwest. Found along virtually all the waterways throughout the region and in RMNP.

Food: Opportunistic—muskrats, mice, fish, birds, frogs, and crayfish.

Nocturnal and solitary, tracks are often the only evidence that mink live in the area. Less aquatic than the otter but more at home in the water than the weasels, mink are never far from the margins of lakes and ponds. Excellent swimmers, they pursue the wide variety of small creatures that inhabit shorelines. Differences in size between males and females result in different prey being taken. The largest prey—muskrats, for example—are usually taken by males, while females hunt correspondingly smaller prey.

Mink often take over a muskrat burrow to use for a den, usually after killing the inhabitant. Breeding, a rough and tumble affair that seems to involve the male subduing the female, occurs about February. Males often mate with more than one female and may remain with the last female bred. The resulting young, usually from two to six, are born the first part of May. Gestation varies from 39 to 76 days but averages about 42 days. Born blind and hairless, young mink weigh about a fifth of an ounce but grow rapidly and open their eyes in about 30 days. The families break up about October, and the young go out on their own.

Mink travel extensively along regular routes. As they go, they leave scats and scents on prominent logs and rocks to advertise their presence. Never in a hurry, their insatiable curiosity causes them to investigate every hole, crack, and crevice they encounter.

Valuable furbearers, mink are widely sought by trappers. Ninety percent of the furs sold today, though, comes from mink farms.

Mink with trout —J. L. Wassink

Mink —J. L. Wassink

Mink by den —J. L. Wassink

Wolverine

Gulo gulo

Description: Superficially resemble a small bear; medium brown to black; light facial mask; light upper body stripe from the shoulder to the rump and tail. Broad head; short, stout neck; heavily muscled body; relatively short legs; large feet; five toes with sharply curved semiretractile claws. Males, 28 to 32 inches long; 7-to-9-inch tail; 35 to 60 pounds. Females slightly smaller, 18 to 22 pounds.

Similar species: none.

Habitat/Distribution: Wolverines are wilderness animals and inhabit the high, forested mountains of the West near timberline. Found primarily in northern Wyoming and eastern Idaho, some individuals may occasionally wander further south.

Food: Virtually everything of suitable size—all mammals except big game; birds, eggs, insects, and berries; carrion (which it can locate under 7 feet of snow.)

The wolverine's foul odor, legendary strength, cantankerous disposition, and fearless character are the stuff legends are made of. They can be a backcountry nuisance, with a tendency to rob traps and break into trappers' cabins and food caches. Exaggeration is common, but if reputation were fact, the wolverine would be the personification of evil.

Solitary and nomadic, wolverines range widely—the males over as many as 250 square miles and the females up to 36 square miles. Boundaries and prominent landmarks are marked with feces, urine, and musk. Although its eyesight is poor, its sense of smell is excellent. Carrion is used extensively and the wolverine's massive skull, strong, thick teeth, and heavy musculature enable it to crush even large bones.

Winters are tough. Dense, stiff, bristlelike hair between the toes helps the wolverine move over snow. Its pelage—short, thick, and uniform on the head but progressively longer toward the rump—is unique in that the guard hair will not collect frost.

Capable of breeding anytime from late spring to early fall, wolverines den in sheltered places. After delayed implantation, the two or three young are born in late winter. A single litter is born every two or three years. The young are yellowish white and blind at birth but grow and mature rapidly, leaving the den when they are between 12 and 14 weeks old.

Wolverine —T. J. Ulrich

Wolverine showing characteristic humped appearance —T. J. Ulrich

Wolverine —T. J. Ulrich

Badger

Taxidea taxus

Description: Stocky, flattened appearance; yellowish gray overall; white stripe down spine; white cheeks; black spot in front of each ear; black feet; long front claws; yellowish belly and tail; heavy body, short legs; 18 to 22 inches long; 4-to-6-inch tail; 13 to 25 pounds.

Similar species: none.

Habitat/Distribution: Look for the badger in open, dry grasslands and deserts throughout the region and in RMNP.

Food: Small rodents—ground squirrels, pocket gophers, and mice; also insects, earthworms, invertebrates, and snakes.

The badger is a digger. Its flattened shape, short, powerful front legs tipped with 1½-inch claws, and tremendous strength combine to make the badger the premier excavator in North America. The badger is reputed to be able to outdig two men with shovels and is capable of digging itself out of sight in a very short time. It uses its digging ability to obtain food by digging out small rodents. An ambitious badger may tear up several square yards of soil while foraging for earthworms, snails, or the larvae of yellow jackets or bumblebees.

Needless to say, badgers dig their own dens, usually in sandy or light soils near open country. The nest is usually from 5 to 20 feet from the entrance. The young, from two to five, are born between February and May. They open their eyes in about a month and are weaned several weeks later. Abandoned badger dens provide homes for numerous other creatures, including burrowing owls, foxes, coyotes, skunks, and even rattlesnakes.

Prior to winter, badgers put on a layer of fat to tide them over when prey is scarce and digging tough. They may sleep through cold periods, but they do not hibernate and must find a steady supply of food.

When threatened, the badger digs a hole, backs into it to protect its backside, and faces its attacker with bared teeth. Few animals are willing to take on these formidable defenses.

Economically, the badger is a mixed bag; it destroys large numbers of rodents, but its burrows are hazardous to farm machinery and sometimes result in broken legs for domestic animals.

Badger —J. L. Wassink

Badger —J. L. Wassink

Badger and rattlesnake —T. J. Ulrich

Western Spotted Skunk　　*Spilogale gracilis*

Description: Black-and-white overall pattern; white spot on forehead; single white spot in front of each ear; four broken white stripes on neck, back, and sides. Tail has a white tip. Pale amber eyeshine. Male, 9 to 13½ inches long; 4½-to-9-inch tail; 1 to 2 pounds. Female, slightly smaller, 10 to 20 ounces.

Similar species: Striped skunk—larger; longer hair; unbroken stripes.

Habitat/Distribution: Found in brushy, sparsely wooded habitats, along streams, among boulders, and on prairies. Found throughout the region and in RMNP except northern Wyoming. Have home ranges of around 160 acres, and in good habitat there may be as many as thirteen or more to the square mile.

Food: Opportunistic and omnivorous—mice, birds, eggs, insects, and carrion.

The smallest of the skunks, spotted skunks are nocturnal and seldom seen. More nomadic than their larger cousin, the striped skunk, they have no permanent den but will hole up almost anywhere—in burrows, beneath buildings, under rock piles, in piles of sawdust, woodchips, or straw, and other similar places. They can climb and will occasionally den in trees.

They breed in September; implantation does not occur until late March. The four to seven young are born 120 days later in May. The young are weaned about seven weeks later.

Winter is a rough time for this small carnivore and it may hole up during periods of bad weather to conserve energy. Usually solitary, except for breeding pairs and family groups, several individuals may den together during lean times.

When threatened, spotted skunks may go through a series of antics to warn the intruder to "back-off." The first signal is usually stamping or patting the ground with their front feet. If that does not have the desired effect, they may rock back on their hindlegs and lunge toward the intruder, bringing the front feet down and then drawing them back. The last warning is a handstand. They may balance on their front legs and walk for several feet toward the intruder with their hindquarters and tail in the air. Apparently, this position is ideal for perfuming the intruder. It is wise to heed the first warning!

Western spotted skunk —J. L. Wassink

Western spotted skunk showing varied stripes —J. L. Wassink

Western spotted skunk testing the wind —J. L. Wassink

Striped Skunk

Mephitis mephitis

Description: Contrasting black-and-white pattern; shiny black fur; white stripes on forehead, back of neck, and sides; fluffy black-and-white tail. Deep amber eyeshine. Male, 13 to 18 inches long; 7-to-10-inch tail; 8 to 12 pounds. Female, slightly smaller, 6 to 10 pounds.

Similar species: Western spotted skunk—smaller; more mottled appearance.

Habitat/Distribution: Found in virtually all habitats throughout the region and in RMNP. One skunk per 10 acres is a high population.

Food: Omnivorous—eats a wide variety of animal and vegetable matter.

The most common and widespread skunk in North America, striped skunks are most often seen along roads. They frequently live in close conjunction with humans and will den almost any-where—ground burrows dug and abandoned by woodchucks or badgers, and beneath buildings, boulders, and piles of debris. A more protected den site is selected during the winter.

Striped skunks breed in February or March and the young are born 63 days later (late April to mid-May) in a nest lined with grass and leaves. The usual litter consists of six to eight young, whose eyes open in 28 days. By late June or July, the youngsters are following their mother in the typical single-file skunk formation.

Excellent diggers, they often use their long front claws to forage in rotting logs or soft ground for mice, eggs, insects, grubs, and berries. When available, carrion is taken readily. Striped skunks love bees and will rob beehives by scratching on the entrance hole and eating the bees as they emerge.

Although striped skunks are usually solitary, several females may den together in winter or with a single male. They do not hibernate but may reduce their activity level during inclement weather.

When threatened, skunks first try to flee. If that avenue is thwarted, they will face the intruder, arch their back, raise their tail, and stamp their front feet. Now is a good time to leave, because the next step is spraying. With the exception of the great horned owl and the automobile, most predators respect the skunk's defenses and so it has few natural enemies.

Both striped and spotted skunks often carry rabies, making it desirable to limit their populations to some extent.

Striped skunk —J. L. Wassink

Striped skunk kits —J. L. Wassink

Albino striped skunk —J. L. Wassink

River Otter

Lutra canadensis

Description: Dark brown fur; long, lithe, cylindrical body; small, broad head; large nose; small, beady eyes; small, rounded ears; long whiskers; thick, furry, tapered tail. Pale amber eyeshine. Males, 20 to 35 inches long; 10-to-18-inch tail; 9 inches high; 15 to 25 pounds. Females, two-thirds the size of males; 10 to 18 pounds.

Similar species: Mink—much smaller. Beaver—flat, scaly tail.

Habitat/Distribution: Along the lakes and streams of the northern part of the region. Reintroduced in several places in Colorado beginning in 1976.

Food: Opportunistic, but feed mostly on aquatic foods—fish, frogs, crayfish, and aquatic invertebrates.

Undoubtedly the most playful of the mammals in the Central Rockies, otters enjoy sliding in mud or snow, diving for and playing with stones, wrestling, and playing tag, hide-and-seek, and "bite-the-tail-on-the-beaver."

Life is not all fun and games, however, even for the otter. They must eat. They locate prey by swimming on the water's surface and searching for movement below them, by diving after fish, and in murky water, using their stiff vibrissae (whiskers) to hunt by feel. With streamlined bodies, small flaps of skin to close their noses when diving, and short, powerful legs equipped with broad feet and webbed toes to power them through the water, river otters are totally at home in aquatic environments.

Throughout most of the year, river otters travel through rivers, streams, and lakes in circular routes that may be 25 miles long, occasionally traveling overland for several miles to reach another lake or stream. Dens are located in the banks of waterways, with the entrance located below the water surface. Social animals, otters are often seen in groups of two or three. They breed in summer and the young (one to five) are born in April or May after a gestation period of 9½ to 10 months.

Otters have luxurious pelage. The heavy coat of long, straight, glistening dark brown guard hairs hides the dense, oily fine underfur with so many thousands of hairs to the square inch that water is unable to penetrate to the otter's skin. The luster, strength, and durability of the otter's coat give it a rating of 100 percent on the furrier's scale—the standard by which all other furs are judged.

River otter portrait —J. L. Wassink

River otter —J. L. Wassink

River otter with fish —T. J. Ulrich

Mountain Lion

Description: Gray to yellowish or reddish brown above, shading to white below; small, rounded head; short muzzle; eyes set forward on the head; small, rounded ears; long, lithe body; long, round, black-tipped tail. Male, 50 to 60 inches long; 24-to-36-inch tail; 26 to 30 inches high; 150 to 190 pounds. Females, slightly smaller, 70 to 120 pounds.

Similar species: none.

Habitat/Distribution: Throughout the mountains, foothills, and canyons of the Central Rockies and RMNP.

Food: Carnivorous—deer, elk, porcupine, mice, rabbits, grouse, and bobcats.

Because mountain lions are so large, even the casual observer knows at first glance that this cat is a formidable predator. Its sharp eyes and keen nose locate prey. Short, muscular legs and a supple body help it take advantage of every shred of available cover during the stalk, and padded feet allow it to move without a sound.

At the end of the stalk, powerful hind legs provide the burst of speed it needs to overtake its prey, and strong shoulders and forelegs help it strike and hold on to the animal. Needlelike retractable claws dig into the sides and back of its prey until long, strong canine teeth and muscular jaws finish the struggle with a swift, bone-crushing bite at the base of the skull that causes almost instant death.

Socially, mountain lions, or cougars, are loners. Only breeding pairs and females with young move together. Each cougar has its own home range and rarely ventures outside it. Males have larger home ranges that may overlap to some degree with the smaller home ranges of the females. Females may come in heat year-round, but in the Central Rockies breeding occurs in winter or early spring. Breeding usually occurs between males and females with overlapping home ranges.

The two to four spotted young are often born in May. The den may be located in a cave, under a rock ledge, or beneath a windfall. The kittens stay with the female for 18 to 22 months, while they learn to hunt and kill for themselves. When pushed out on their own, they roam nomadically in search of a suitable, unoccupied home range. It is these wandering juveniles that most often get in trouble by wandering into suburbs and preying on pets or livestock.

Mountain lion —T. J. Ulrich

Mountain lion with an itch —J. L. Wassink

Mountain lion resting —J. L. Wassink

Lynx

Felis lynx

Description: Gray or yellowish gray above; gray belly with faint dark spots; tufted ears edged in black; prominent "sideburns"; gray tail circled at the tip with black; long, unspotted legs; extremely large feet. Male, 32 to 36 inches long; 4-inch tail; 20 to 30 pounds. Female, slightly smaller, 15 to 25 pounds.

Similar species: Bobcat—smaller; tail black on top side only.

Habitat/Distribution: Dense coniferous forest, with small clearings and stands of spruce/fir on cold, north slopes, over 9,000 feet. Found in high mountains along Wyoming/Idaho border; not documented in Utah, scattered records in Colorado.

Food: Snowshoe hares; also mice, voles, red squirrels, flying squirrels, ruffed grouse, and ptarmigan; scavenge on big game.

Lynx are well suited for preying on snowshoe hares, which make up over half of their diet. They eat an average of two snowshoes every three days, which are caught either by flushing the hares from thick cover and running them down or by waiting in ambush near heavily used snowshoe hare trails.

Lynx numbers cycle with those of snowshoe hares in a predator-prey-forage relationship that is really quite simple. With an abundance of food available during high snowshoe populations, lynx have large litters and kitten survival rate is high. The abundant snowshoes eventually overuse their food supply and their numbers drop. Predation by the large lynx population hastens the decline. As their prey base declines, lynx cannot find enough alternate prey and both litter size and kitten survival rates begin dropping. Fewer lynx result in lower predation levels that, coupled with recovering forage, allow snowshoe numbers to increase. With more snowshoes around, lynx litter size and survival rates increase and the cycle continues.

In winter, when snow impedes movement, the very similar bobcat moves to areas with less snow. Not the lynx. Longer legs and broad paws, which support twice as much weight as those of the bobcat, help the lynx move through deep snow and at least partially explain why lynx are found in areas with greater winter snow depths than the bobcat.

Human activities that open up forests and encourage the brushy undergrowth used by deer, moose, and snowshoe rabbits also benefit lynx. Encroaching civilization will nevertheless continue to reduce lynx numbers, even without hunting or trapping.

Lynx —T. J. Ulrich

Lynx kitten —T. J. Ulrich

Lynx chasing snowshoe —T. J. Ulrich

Bobcat

Felis rufus

Description: Spotted body and legs; more reddish in color than the lynx; ear tufts and sideburns short; black on tail only on top half; feet smaller than the lynx. Male, 25 to 30 inches long; 5-inch tail; 20 to 35 pounds. Female, slightly smaller, 15 to 25 pounds.

Similar species: Lynx—larger; tail circled at tip with black.

Habitat/Distribution: Dry rock mountainsides, shrubland, coniferous forests, broken rocky country throughout the region and in RMNP.

Food: Mostly rabbits and hares, also ground squirrels, mice, birds, insects, lizards, crayfish, and frogs.

The most common cat in the region, the bobcat is shy and furtive, moving about in thick vegetation or under the cover of darkness. It flourishes in the broken, semiwild areas left by logging, burning, and other human activities.

Efficient predators, they locate prey in poor light with eyes that are almost six times as acute as our own or with ears that are especially sensitive to high-frequency sound, such as the squeak of a mouse.

Once located, the prey is stalked or taken from ambush. Powerful legs give the bobcat blinding speed over short distances. If the prey is not overtaken with a short dash, the cat breaks off pursuit and searches for another animal. Once overtaken, the prey is caught and held by razor-sharp retractable front claws and then dispatched with a bone-crushing bite behind the neck.

The social system of bobcats is similar to that of the cougar, with overlapping home ranges and breeding between males and females whose home ranges overlap. Possession of a home range is maintained by a system of scent and visual signals. The resident bobcat squirts urine along travel routes and makes scrapes at trail intersections and at other important locations in the home range to advertise his presence. An intruding cat that comes upon these marks usually respects the territorial rights of the resident and moves on.

Kittens are raised in caves or some similar location. At about 17 days, they begin to play with each other. The playing gets progressively rougher and soon includes mock fighting. These rough-and-tumble games sharpen reflexes and develop strength to prepare the kittens for life on their own.

Bobcat —T. J. Ulrich

Bobcat kittens —T. J. Ulrich

Bobcat —J. L. Wassink

Order Rodentia
Rodents

Most of the mammals in the Central Region, as in the world, are rodents. The common characteristic among them is the presence of four incisor teeth that are used for gnawing. The incisors grow throughout the lifetime of the rodent but are kept to an optimal length by being worn down through chewing.

Rodents vary widely in size, from the 40-pound beaver to the 2-ounce mice and voles. They also vary widely in form and may live on dry land, underground, in the water, or in trees. Generalized descriptions of families of rodents found in the Central Rockies are given below.

Family Sciuridae: Chipmunks, marmots, ground squirrels, tree squirrels, flying squirrels, and prairie dogs. With the exception of the flying squirrel, all are diurnal (active during the day). They have bushy tails, four toes on the front feet and five on the back.

Family Geomyidae: Pocket gophers. They are subterranean and specialized for living underground.

Family Heteromyidae: Pocket mice, kangaroo mice, and kangaroo rats. These rodents are small, have fur-lined cheek pouches, long, powerful hind legs, and live in arid or semi-arid habitats.

Family Zapodidae: Jumping mice. They have long tails and large hind feet, but no cheek pouches.

Family Castoridae: Beaver. Beaver are the largest rodents in the region and specialized for a semi-aquatic lifestyle.

Family Cricetidae: Mice, voles, woodrats, and the muskrat. They are small to medium in size and have large ears, large eyes, and long (rarely bushy) tails.

Family Muridae: Old World mice and rats. They were imported accidentally and live in and around human habitations.

Family Erethizontidae: Porcupine. Distinguished by the presence of sharp quills.

Rodent incisors —J. L. Wassink

Black-tailed prairie dog —J. L. Wassink

Muskrat —J. L. Wassink

Porcupine —J. L. Wassink

Hibernation and Estivation

True hibernation, sometimes called "little death," is the ultimate in energy conservation and occurs only in certain warm-blooded animals of medium size, such as marmots and ground squirrels.

Like the bears, hibernators spend the fall gorging and building up a layer of fat to sustain them during the winter and early spring. As the time for hibernation approaches, they become lethargic and then disappear underground, not to reappear until spring.

Once underground, they undergo dramatic physiological changes. The body temperature of a ground squirrel will drop from around 89 degrees Fahrenheit to about 42 degrees Fahrenheit. Its respiration rate drops from around 100 breaths per minute to about 4 per minute, and its heart rate drops from about 250 beats per minute to around 10 beats per minute. Brain waves become slow and irregular; electrical activity in the brain may drop 90 percent, and some areas of the brain appear to shut down altogether. The blood vessels in the rear end of the animal constrict, concentrating the blood in the areas more vulnerable to cold and oxygen deficiency, such as the heart and brain. Levels of magnesium and a chemical called "noradrenaline" increase throughout the body.

These changes effectively anesthetize the animal, making it possible to handle it without waking it. An interesting side effect of these physiological changes is a drastic reduction in the clotting time of the blood. An animal cut while hibernating will scarcely bleed. Once hibernation begins, the animal does not change position or stir until spring, when its internal clock wakens it by reversing the changes that took place in the fall.

Yellow-bellied marmot —J. L. Wassink

Chipmunks

Description: Colors range from chestnut to yellowish gray to light gray; lighter below; striped face; dark median stripe along the back to the base of the tail with two parallel stripes; 3½ to 6 inches long; 3-to-4½ inch tail; 1 to 4 ounces.

Food: Vegetation—stems, buds, seeds, leaves, flowers, and fruits from a wide variety of plants. Insects make up almost 50 percent of the diet of the least chipmunk, much more than any other chipmunk.

The smallest of the squirrels, chipmunks are quick, active rodents with internal cheek pouches that they use to carry food. They climb readily but never go far above the ground. They are active only during the day and hibernate in winter. Burrows are excavated under rocks, logs, and roots, dug to below frostline. The grass-lined nest will be home to one or two litters of four to six young.

Chipmunks are difficult to identify and the generalized description given above fits them all. When trying to identify a particular species, the habitat where it is seen is important. In locations where more than one species is found, subtle differences in coloration, size, and behavior are used to identify the species. When precise identification is a must, the skull must be examined.

Least Chipmunk   *Tamias minimus*

Habitat / Distribution: It can be seen from the low sagebrush deserts at lower elevations to the high mountain coniferous forests. The most wide-ranging of the chipmunks, it is found throughout the region and in RMNP. Tail held straight up when running.

Cliff Chipmunk   *Tamias dorsalis*

Habitat / Distribution: Frequents rocky outcrops in piñon/juniper, scrub oak, and mountain mahogany habitats in a limited area in southern Wyoming, the northwest corner of Colorado, and eastern Utah. Not found in RMNP.

Colorado Chipmunk   *Tamias quadrivittatus*

Habitat / Distribution: Inhabits piñon, piñon/juniper, scrub oak, and mountain mahogany habitats south of the Wyoming border and in RMNP.

Uinta Chipmunk   *Tamias umbrinus*

Habitat / Distribution: Found in subalpine fir, lodgepole pine, and Douglas fir habitats in eastern Utah, northern Colorado, and RMNP.

Yellow Pine Chipmunk   *Tamias amoenus*

Habitat / Distribution: Found in western Wyoming and eastern Utah. Not found in Colorado or Utah or RMNP.

Chipmunk —J. L. Wassink

Chipmunk —J. L. Wassink

Chipmunk —J. L. Wassink

Yellow-bellied Marmot   *Marmota flaviventris*

Description: Brown to yellowish brown above; yellowish below; white patch between the eyes; conspicuous buffy patches on sides of neck; heavy body; short legs; 14 to 20 inches long; 5-to-7-inch tail; 5 to 10 pounds.

Habitat/Distribution: Found throughout the region in rocky habitats—talus slopes, valleys and foothills, pastures with large boulders.

Food: Mostly grasses but some other plant materials.

Usually first seen lounging atop the large boulders that protect their dens, yellow-bellied marmots live in loose colonies of up to two dozen individuals. When not sunbathing, they may venture far from the shelter of their burrows to feed on grasses and alfalfa. Foxes, coyotes, badgers, and golden eagles will consume any marmot that they catch away from the den; however, with at least one marmot perched on a rock looking out for danger, that does not happen often. At the first sign of a disturbance, the lookout emits a series of high-pitched chirps to warn nearby marmots of danger.

The largest ground-dwelling squirrel in the region, marmots may escape the heat of the summer by going into estivation in July and beginning hibernation in September. Since they do not emerge from hibernation until March or April, they may spend as much as eight months a year underground.

Three to six young are born in late April or May. Naked and blind at birth, they mature quickly and emerge from the den about a month later. They are fully grown by the end of August but go into hibernation later than the adults, presumably because it takes them longer to lay on the necessary layer of fat. In addition, after leaving the home den, they must locate a den of their own and prepare it for winter by lining it with grasses. They will breed as adults when they emerge the following spring.

Marmots near agricultural areas may feast on garden vegetables, alfalfa, and other croplands where they are not wanted. Under most circumstances, people enjoy seeing these intriguing mammals and hearing their clear-toned whistle.

Yellow-bellied marmot —J. L. Wassink

Yellow-bellied marmot —J. L. Wassink

Young yellow-bellied marmots —J. L. Wassink

Ground Squirrels voice a high-pitched chirp. They often estivate in July/August and hibernate from August/September to February/March. Young (two to ten) are born in April or May after about a month's gestation. Most species feed on green vegetation in spring and early summer and on seeds later in the year. All the ground squirrels are important prey species for a wide variety of mammalian and avian predators.

Uinta
Ground Squirrel *Spermophilus armatus*

Description: Brownish above; buff below; tail black to buffy white above; buffy white below; 8 to 9 inches long; 3-inch tail; 10 to 15 ounces.

Similar Species: Richardson's Ground Squirrel—tail with light borders.

Habitat/Distribution: Found in open country with green vegetation, such as meadows and field borders, up to 8,000 feet in elevation in extreme western Wyoming, eastern Idaho, and northern Utah; not found in Colorado.

In spring, the males emerge a couple of weeks before the females. Breeding takes place soon after emergence and the young are born when there is an abundance of tender green plants. These squirrels rely on green vegetation more than some of the other ground squirrels. They live in colonies.

Richardson's
Ground Squirrel *Spermophilus richardsonii*

Description: Smoke-gray with a cinnamon-buff tint; may be faintly spotted above; pale buff or white below; borders and underside of tail buff or light brown; 8 to 10 inches long; 2-to-4-inch tail; 10 to 18 ounces.

Similar Species: Uinta Ground Squirrel—tail black with white-tipped hairs.

Habitat/Distribution: Sagebrush and grassland with green vegetation, up to 11,000-foot level. Western Wyoming, northern half of Colorado.

Richardson's ground squirrels often feed on carrion as well as green vegetation. Burrows are often located near others of their species and may have several entrances. Even though they hibernate, they also store seeds and other food in their burrows. Where they live near agricultural crops, they may cause some damage.

Uinta ground squirrel
—J. L. Wassink

Richardson's ground squirrel
—J. L. Wassink

Young Richardson's ground squirrel —J. L. Wassink

Thirteen-lined
Ground Squirrel
Spermophilus tridecemlineatus

Description: Light to dark brown with 13 whitish stripes on sides and back; whitish below; 4 to 7 inches long; 3-to-5-inch tail; 5 to 9 ounces.

Similar Species: Chipmunks—stripes on face.

Habitat/Distribution: Found in suitable habitat throughout the region except extreme western Wyoming, Idaho, and southwestern Colorado.

In addition to green vegetation, they feed on insects and seeds, and eat more meat than other ground squirrels. Unlike most of the other ground squirrels, they are solitary rather than colonial and do not pile dirt around the entrance holes to their burrows. The burrow usually consists of a short, vertical shaft that flattens out into several side branches, ending in a nesting chamber and several storage rooms. They may have more than one burrow—a shallow one that is used in summer and a deeper one that is used during the winter hibernation.

Golden-mantled
Ground Squirrel
Spermophilus lateralis

Description: Coppery head and neck; gray back; whitish sides with one or two black stripes that do not extend to the face or the tail; tail gray above, lighter below; 6 to 8 inches long; 2-to-5-inch tail; 6 to 10 ounces.

Similar species: Chipmunks—stripes extend to face.

Habitat/Distribution: Frequents the alpine tundra, subalpine fir, lodgepole pine, piñon, juniper, mountain mahogany, and aspen habitats throughout the region and in RMNP. Not found in the desert habitats of southwestern Utah.

The golden-mantled ground squirrel feeds on a variety of vegetation—fruits and seeds—as well as insects and some meat. When an abundance of food is available, they may store some of it. Like the other grounds squirrels, they burrow under rocks, logs, roots, and bushes. True hibernators, they disappear around October, and in areas where winter hangs on, they may not reappear until May. The two to eight young are born in early spring. Quite protective, the female may defend the area around the den.

Common in many parks and campgrounds, golden-mantled ground squirrels become accustomed to people and may beg for handouts. Obliging them is illegal in national parks and bad for their health anywhere.

Thirteen-lined ground squirrel —J. L. Wassink

Golden-mantled ground squirrel —J. L. Wassink
Golden-mantled ground squirrel —J. L. Wassink

Black-tailed Prairie Dog

Cynomys ludovicianus

Description: Brownish yellow back and sides; whitish below; small ears; last third of tail black; 11 to 12 inches long; 1-to-2½-inch tail; 1½ to 2½ pounds.

Similar Species: White-tailed Prairie Dog—tip of tail is white.

Habitat/Distribution: Found in the dry plains at lower elevations along the eastern edge of the region. Not found in RMNP.

Food: Primarily grasses but also insects, especially grasshoppers.

The most common and widespread of the prairie dogs, black-tailed prairie dogs dig elaborate burrows in colonies called "towns" which they defend against neighboring towns. Usually one or more watch for predators while the others feed. If a predator is seen, the sentinel sounds a warning bark that is repeated throughout the town, and all the "dogs" disappear down their burrows. During cold weather, they may stay underground for long periods of time, but do not hibernate. Black-tailed prairie dogs are sometimes still persecuted because they compete with domestic livestock for grass.

White-tailed Prairie Dog

Cynomys leucurus

Description: Brownish yellow back and sides; whitish below; small ears; tip of tail is white; 11 to 12 inches long; 1-to-2½-inch tail; 1½ to 2½ pounds.

Similar Species: Black-tailed prairie dog—tip of tail is black.

Habitat/Distribution: Dry mountain valleys, open country, scattered juniper, and pine habitats at higher elevations (5,000 to 8,000 feet) throughout most of the region except northwestern Wyoming and Idaho; not found in RMNP.

Food: Grasses and some insects.

Less colonial and found at higher elevations than the black-tailed prairie dogs, white-tailed "dogs" may estivate in July. Also unlike the black-tail, they may hibernate from October to March with the young of the year entering the burrows with the adults. They mate shortly after emerging in the spring, and the three to five young are born in early May. Their burrows are used by burrowing owls, rattlesnakes, and a great many other creatures.

Black-tailed prairie dog —J. L. Wassink

Black-tailed prairie dog —J. L. Wassink

White-tailed prairie dog —J. L. Wassink

White-tailed prairie dog —J. L. Wassink

Abert's Squirrel

Sciurus aberti

Description: Black, gray, or reddish sides; white or black belly; tail black above, white below, or all black; conspicuous ear tassels; 11 to 12 inches long; 8-to-9-inch tail; 1½ to 2 pounds.

Habitat/Distribution: Found in the yellow pine forests of Colorado and east-central Utah from 7,000 to 8,500 feet, and in RMNP.

Very dependent on ponderosa pine trees, these squirrels feed on the pinecones, the sweet inner bark of the small twigs, the buds, and fungi growing in and around the trees. They nest in them, hide in them to avoid predators, and use them for courting and raising their young.

Fox Squirrel

Sciurus niger

Description: Yellowish or orangish brown above, lighter yellowish or orangish below; bushy tail with fulvous edges; 10 to 15 inches long; 9-to-14-inch tail; 1¼ to 3 pounds.

Habitat/Distribution: Introduced in various cities and towns throughout the region.

A very common and important game animal in the East, the fox squirrel has been extending its range to the west, primarily along river bottoms. Introductions by squirrel lovers have speeded the range extension. More heavy-bodied than the native squirrels, and therefore less agile in the trees, fox squirrels spend a lot of time on the ground in search of nuts, acorns, seeds, fungi, and eggs. They nest in cavities or in nests built of leaves and twigs in the crotch of a tree.

Fox squirrel feeding on Russian olive —J. L. Wassink

Abert's squirrel —W. Shattil & R. Rozinsky

Red Squirrel
Tamiasciurus hudsonicus

Description: Uniform yellowish or reddish brown above; whitish below; black line along side in summer; bushy tail; 7 to 8 inches long; 4-to-6-inch tail; 7 to 9 ounces.

Habitat/Distribution: Pine and spruce forests throughout the region and in RMNP.

The most common and widespread squirrel in the region, red squirrels feed on a wide variety of seeds, nuts, eggs, and fungi. They store conifer cones and nuts in caches, and fungi in tree crotches. They often have a favorite feeding stump or branch, resulting in a large accumulation of cone scales beneath it. Nests are located in a tree cavity or are outside nests built with leaves, twigs, and shredded bark, providing shelter for two litters of young each year, April-May and August-September.

Red squirrel —J. L. Wassink

Northern
Flying Squirrel

Glaucomys sabrinus

Description: Thick, glossy brown fur above; white below; loose flap of skin along sides, from the front and back legs. Reddish orange eyeshine; 5½ to 6½ inches long; 4-to-5½-inch tail; 4 to 6½ ounces.

Habitat/Distribution: Coniferous forests of western Wyoming, eastern Idaho, and northern Utah. Not found in Colorado or RMNP.

Food: Seeds, nuts, eggs, and insects. Will also eat meat when available. Caches food in nest cavity and in crotches of trees. Frequently seen visiting bird feeders just after dark.

Although flying squirrels are very common and in suitable habitat may actually outnumber their more boisterous cousin, the red squirrel, relatively few people have seen these little creatures. The only nocturnal squirrel in the region, they do not emerge from their den tree until after dusk, well after most humans have left the woods. After a little preliminary gliding, they settle down to their nightly search for food.

The flight of the flying squirrel is actually a glide, made possible by flaps of skin between the forelimbs and hindlimbs. There is a slender cartilage at each wrist that projects outward when the forelimb is extended, thus stretching the gliding membrane between the limbs. When gliding, the squirrel appears almost square and flat except for the long, flattened, feather-shaped tail.

Before takeoff, the squirrel bobs its head up and down and then from side to side, presumably to aid in distance perception. When all is ready, the squirrel launches itself with all four feet, spreads its "wings" and "flies." Once airborne, the direction of the glide is controlled by the forelimbs. The distance of the glide depends solely on the height of the take-off. Although flights of over 300 feet have been recorded, 50 or 60 feet are more common.

Sometime in June, two to seven young are born in a tree cavity, an outside nest of leaves, twigs, and bark, or in a convenient attic. Born pink, blind, and hairless, the young nurse every few hours and grow rapidly. At about six weeks, the young squirrels begin stretching their "wings."

Northern flying squirrel —J. L. Wassink

Northern flying squirrel landing on den tree —J. L. Wassink

Northern flying squirrel in winter den —J. L. Wassink

Family Geomyidae

The family **Geomyidae** consists of only the pocket gophers—small-to-medium-sized mammals (5 to 6½ inches long; 1½-to-3-inch tail; 2½ to 4½ ounces) that spend almost their entire lives underground. They are grayish brown with lighter bellies. Living underground as they do, they have no need for keen sight or hearing, and their eyes and ears are small. Their incisors are yellowish and always exposed. External fur-lined cheek pouches open on either side of the mouth and can be turned inside out. Strong front feet and long, curved front claws make them efficient diggers. The tail is short and almost hairless.

Although they are seldom seen, the presence of pocket gophers is easily detected. While excavating their tunnels, dirt is packed into the cheek pouches and carried to the surface where it is deposited in mounds. The mound marks the outside entrance to the tunnel system. Because they spend their whole life digging, they find life easier in slightly moist soil, where digging is less strenuous.

Pocket gophers are solitary for most of their lives. Protected from the weather and predators by the earth, they are active both day and night throughout the year. They may tunnel through the snow in winter, leaving loose ribbons of dirt on the surface of the ground when the snow melts. Pocket gophers feed mostly on tubers and roots and sometimes on surface vegetation. The roots and tubers are obtained by burrowing just below the surface of the ground. Surface vegetation may be munched from aboveground but may also be pulled down through the soil into the burrows.

The breeding biology of the pocket gopher is not well known. They have four to seven young, born between February and June, and may have two litters per year.

Pocket gopher species look very similar and are difficult to differentiate by sight. Perhaps the best way for the novice to identify the species is by its range. The **Northern Pocket Gopher** (*Thomomys talpoides*) is found in grassy areas of alpine meadows, brushy habitats, and open pine forests throughout the region and in RMNP. When found in close proximity to other species of pocket gophers, this species is found higher in the mountains. Other pocket gophers in the region include **Botta's Pocket Gopher** (*Thomomys bottae*), found in eastern Utah and southern and western Colorado, and the **Plains Pocket Gopher** (*Geomys bursarius*), found along the eastern edge of the region.

Northern pocket gopher —A. G. Nelson

Pocket gopher workings —T. J. Ulrich

The family **Heteromyidae** includes the pocket mice, kangaroo rats, and kangaroo mice. These small mammals have fur-lined cheek pouches that open on either side of the mouth. They have relatively weak front legs, long, strong hind legs, and tails that are longer than the body. Adapted to dry conditions, they do not need free water, but obtain their water from the metabolism of their food. Because they burrow, they prefer light, sandy soils.

Hispid Pocket Mouse *Perognathus hispidus*

Description: Yellowish buff mixed with black; white below; long tail; 4 to 5 inches in length; 3 to 5 inch tail; 1 to 2 ounces.

Habitat/Distribution: Found along eastern edge of the region along margins of short grass prairie. Not found in RMNP.

Food: Seeds and insects.

The entrances to the rather complex burrow systems of these nocturnal mammals go straight down and usually lack a tell-tale pile of dirt. Pocket mice do not hibernate and may have their young at anytime of year. In the northern extent of their range, they may have two litters per year; in the south, they may have as many as six litters.

Ord's Kangaroo Rat *Dipodomys ordii*

Description: Brownish gray above; pale below; long tail with tuft on end; white stripe along each side; 4 to 5 inches long; 5-to-6-inch tail; 1½ to 2½ ounces.

Habitat/Distribution: Found in arid and semi-arid habitats throughout the region. Not found in RMNP.

Food: Seeds, forbs, grasses, and some insects.

Ord's kangaroo rat stores seeds underground. It is nocturnal and active throughout the year, drinking water when available. Two to five young are born in May or June, and there may be two litters each year.

Hispid pocket mouse —W. Shattil & R. Rozinski

Ord's kangaroo rat —W. Shattil & R. Rozinski

Family Castoridae

The family **Castoridae** has only one member in North America—the beaver. The beaver is the largest rodent in North America, and frontiersmen pursuing its valuable pelts had a large influence on the settlement of the West.

Beaver   *Castor canadensis*

Description: Rich, brown fur; chunky body; huge yellowish front teeth; naked, scaly, paddle-shaped tail; 25 to 30 inches long; 9-to-10-inch tail; 30 to 60 pounds.

Similar Species: River otter—streamlined body; round tail covered with fur. Muskrat—smaller; tail naked but not paddle-shaped.

Habitat/Distribution: Lakes, ponds, and slow-moving rivers throughout the region and in RMNP.

Food: Bark and small twigs of aspen, alder, willow, birch, cottonwood, poplar, and maple trees.

The beaver was made for the water. Its large, chunky body, dense waterproof fur, and subcutaneous layer of fat minimize heat loss to icy water. A transparent eyelid protects the eyes, and the ear and nose openings can be closed while the animal is underwater. Adaptations of the respiratory and circulatory systems increase their efficiency. Large, webbed feet and powerful hind legs further enhance its underwater abilities.

One of the few animals besides man that modifies its environment to any great degree, beaver build dams of sticks and mud across streams and slow rivers. After felling trees along the banks, cutting them into small sections and eating the bark, the stripped sticks are woven into the dam and held in place with mud. They also build large cone-shaped lodges, either in deep water or near the bank. The entrance is underwater but the nest chamber is well above the waterline.

The lodge is occupied by a breeding pair, yearlings, and kits (young of the year). The two to four young are born, fully furred and with their eyes open, sometime between April and July. When the young are two years old, they either leave on their own or are driven out by the adults. Until they disperse and start their own colonies, all members of the colony help maintain the dam and build the food cache of sticks and logs that will sustain the colony through the winter.

Beaver —T. J. Ulrich

Beaver —T. J. Ulrich

Beaver pond and lodge —T. J. Ulrich

The family **Cricetidae** includes small-to-medium-sized rodents (2 to 10 inches long) except for the muskrat, which may reach 14 inches. Most have four toes on the front feet, some have five, but all have five toes on the hind feet. Tails are covered with hair but not bushy. Some members (mice and rats) have large eyes and ears, and long tails. Others (voles) have small eyes and ears, and short tails. They live in a wide variety of habitats and there is no place in the Central Rockies that does not have one or more members of this family present.

Deer Mouse *Peromyscus maniculatus*

Description: Grayish to reddish brown above; tail sharply bicolored—dark above, white below; 2½ to 4 inches long; 2-to-5-inch tail; ½ to 1¼ ounces.

Similar Species: White-footed mouse—tail not sharply bicolored. Canyon mouse—extremely long tail, fur long. Brush mouse—extremely long tail. Piñon mouse and rock mouse—large ears; sharply bicolored tail.

Habitat/Distribution: The most widely distributed and common Peromyscus in the region. Virtually every dry-land habitat within the region—forests, grasslands, and mixed habitats. Common to abundant throughout the region and in RMNP.

Food: Lives on seeds, nuts, and insects. Will store food when excess is available.

If adaptability to its habitat is the animal criterion for success, then the deer mouse is the most successful animal in the region. Even though it is the most abundant and widespread mammal in the Rockies, it is active primarily at night and so is seldom seen. They build their nests in burrows in the ground, beneath rocks, in logs, trees, buildings, or almost any other protected area. They forage home ranges that may vary in size from one-third acre to over three acres. Although they do store some food, this instinct is not as strong in the deer mouse as it is in some of the other mice.

They breed from April to September. Because females are polyestrous and go into heat after giving birth, they are pregnant almost constantly during the warm part of the year. Litter size varies from one to nine, usually five. Gestation, usually 24 days, extends to 34 days if the female is lactating. Young females will breed at four weeks, males at six weeks.

Because of their abundance, deer mice are an important part of the Central Rockies ecosystems. They provide food for both mammalian and avian predators. Even if they manage to escape predators, they rarely live over two years in the wild.

Deer mouse —J. L. Wassink

Deer mouse —J. L. Wassink

Young deer mouse —W. Shattil & R. Rozinski

Bushy-tailed Woodrat   *Neotoma cinerea*

Description: Brown above; white below; large eyes; big ears; long whiskers; bushy, long-haired tail; 7 to 10 inches long; 5-to-8-inch tail; 7 to 21 ounces.

Similar species: White-throated woodrat—tail not long-haired.

Habitat/Distribution: Inhabits rock slides, cliffs, canyon caves, and rocky ledges in the arid, forested, and rocky areas throughout the region and in RMNP.

Food: Leaves, seeds, stems, berries, and fungi; also insects and carrion. Because they are active all year, they gather and store food in fall for winter use.

The presence of the bushy-tailed woodrat is most easily detected by its large, ramshackle nest, which resembles a mass of debris left by floodwaters. Built with sticks, weathered bones, woodchips and splinters, bits of bark, dung, and stones, a newly constructed nest may measure 5 feet across and 2 feet high. While the jumble of sticks looks haphazard, scientists believe that it may moderate the air temperature of the interior. The sleeping chamber, a neat ball of soft material consisting of feathers, bits of animal hair, and grasses, is buried deep in the ramshackle structure. The nest also contains an area for food storage and another for a latrine.

Following the early spring breeding season, two to four young woodrats are born. The young nurse for the first two or three weeks of life, aided by specially developed teeth that help them grasp their mother's nipples.

Extremely agile, woodrats can climb, run, and jump with the best. Instilled with an uncontrollable urge to carry things in their mouths, they often pick up stones, sticks, or similar objects while coming and going from their nests. Unable to distinguish between worthless objects and those of value to other creatures, such as humans, these packrats will carry away rolls of film, small knives, mouse traps, jewelry, spectacles, sticks of dynamite, silverware, and even dentures—sometimes leaving behind a stick, stone, or similar object. The packrat is not being fairminded but simply impulsive. If, while carrying something in its mouth, the animal spots another, more interesting item, it will drop whatever it is carrying and pick up the more intriguing object. This habit, and the sometimes unbelievable volume of junk collected by these critters, has resulted in the nickname "packrat."

Bushy-tailed woodrat near nest —J. L. Wassink

Bushy-tailed woodrat —J. L. Wassink

Bushy-tailed woodrat with poptop tab —J. L. Wassink

Voles have relatively inconspicuous ears, small eyes, and bluntly rounded muzzles. Inhabitants of moist areas, they feed almost exclusively on the green parts of grasses, sedges, and other succulent plants. They construct runways through vegetation by chewing plants off at the bases. Their snug nests, located along these runways, may be found either above or below ground level. The young (three to five) may be born any time of year and several litters per year are common.

Although they are most active at night, voles do move around during the day. Because they rarely leave the protection of their runways, this daytime activity does not expose them to predation as much as one might think. Their reluctance to leave their runways has forced the predators that hunt them extensively, such as foxes, coyotes, weasels, owls, and harriers, to locate them by sound rather than sight.

Very prolific, voles become sexually active during the season in which they are born. Over a six-month period, with an average of four young per litter and without loss to predation or disease, a single pair of voles in a field could multiply to over 170 individuals—a phenomenon worthy of being called a "population explosion." There are records of population booms occurring in other regions that have resulted in between 8,000 and 12,000 voles per acre of ground in certain agricultural districts—a situation resulting from few or no predators and an abundant food supply.

Meadow Vole   *Microtus pennsylvanicus*

Description: Grayish brown above; silvery belly; dark, beady eyes; ears small and inconspicuous; short, bicolored tail; 3½ to 5 inches long; 1½-to-2½-inch tail; 1 to 2½ ounces.

Habitat/Distribution: From low, moist habitats to high grasslands with thick grassy cover, often near water. Found throughout the region and in RMNP.

Food: Grasses, seeds, grain, bark, and insects. May damage young trees by girdling while feeding on the bark.

Montane Vole   *Microtus montanus*

Description: Grayish brown to blackish above; whitish belly; dark, beady eyes; small, inconspicuous ears; short tail; 4 to 5½ inches long; 1-to-2½-inch-tail; 1 to 3 ounces.

Habitat/Distribution: Same habitats as the meadow vole but found higher in the mountain valleys.

Food: Grasses, sedges, seeds, bark, and insects.

Meadow vole —J. L. Wassink

Young montane vole —J. L. Wassink
Vole castings —J. L. Wassink

Muskrat
Ondatra zibethicus

Description: Rich brown coat of dense fur; gray below; long, naked, scaly tail flattened from side to side; 10 to 14 inches long; 8-to-11-inch tail; 2 to 4 pounds.

Similar species: Beaver—larger; large, flat paddle-shaped tail.

Habitat/Distribution: Found near cattails and rushes in slow rivers, streams, ponds, lakes, and marshes throughout the region and in RMNP.

Food: Aquatic vegetation—cattails, bulrushes, sedges, duckweed; also some invertebrates; fish, frogs, and salamanders; crayfish, clams, and mussels.

Semiaquatic like the beaver, the muskrat has many similar adaptations. Special flaps of skin close off the mouth behind the incisors to allow the muskrat to cut and dig submerged food without getting water in its mouth. Hair webs between the toes of the hind feet aid in propulsion, and the laterally flattened tail is used as a rudder. The muskrat often stays underwater for five minutes at a time and is known to have remained submerged for more than fifteen minutes.

When living in standing water, muskrats pile marsh vegetation into conical mounds in one to three feet of water. They then cut out tunnels and a nesting chamber to live in. Where they live in moving water, which would erode the usual hut, they burrow into mud banks. In either case, the entrance is located underwater. Feeding platforms may also be built.

Each hut or den is occupied by a single family group consisting of a breeding pair and their young. Iceout in the spring signals both the onset of the breeding season and the dispersal of the young still living in the den.

Many muskrats are monogamous. The male stays with the female until just before the young are born, when she drives him out. The litter of five or six young are born in 30 days. Naked, blind, and helpless at birth, their eyes open at 14 days, they are weaned at 24 days, and on their own after a month. The female can breed again immediately after giving birth, so the new litter is born soon after the first young are fully grown. A pair of adults may have two or three litters each year.

Once a valuable fur animal, their hides are not in demand at present. Their main enemies are mink and man, but they are also taken by other mammalian predators, as well as avian hunters.

Muskrat —T. J. Ulrich

Muskrat —J. L. Wassink

Muskrat hut in frozen pond —J. L. Wassink

Aggressive colonizers, these rodents probably left Europe with Columbus in the holds of the *Niña,* the *Pinta,* and the *Santa Maria.* There they passed the long voyage munching on the rations intended for the explorers in the new country. When the ships landed, the mice and rats were transported to land along with the food and grain. With an entire continent just waiting, over the centuries the newcomers quietly boarded wagons, saddlebags, rucksacks, and eventually trains and trucks. They set up housekeeping wherever the ride stopped and can now be found in pantrys and granaries throughout the New World. The result has been a love-hate relationship with humans—they love us for providing them with food and shelter, while we hate them for being ugly, presumptuous, and messy guests.

Norway Rat *Rattus norvegicus*

Description: Grayish brown above; lighter gray below; long, naked, scaly tail; 7 to 10 inches long; 5-to-8-inch tail; 7 to 10 ounces.

Similar Species: Woodrats—white below; tails not naked.

Habitat/Distribution: Colonial and found only near human habitations, the Norway rat burrows around foundations and beneath trash piles, or simply moves into buildings. Lives only near cities and farmyards in the region.

Food: Will eat anything edible.

Norway rats can reproduce rapidly, with up to ten young per litter and up to twelve litters per year. Gestation is about 21 days and females breed at three months. These animals destroy millions of dollars' worth of food, grain, and other goods each year and are carriers of many communicable diseases.

House Mouse *Mus musculus*

Description: Grayish brown above; slightly lighter gray below; long, scaly, uniformly colored tail; 3 to 3½ inches long; 3-to-4-inch tail; ⅓ to 1 ounce.

Similar Species: Deer mouse—white belly; bicolored tail. Voles—short tail.

Habitat/Distribution: Houses or outbuildings but may occasionally venture into nearby grainfields. Found near humans throughout the region and in RMNP.

Food: Anything edible.

The house mouse is very prolific. Three to eleven young are born in each of several litters each year. Breed at six weeks.

Norway rat —J. L. Wassink

House mouse —J. L. Wassink

Young house mice —J. L. Wassink

Porcupine

Family Erethizontidae
Erethizon dorsatum

Description: Large; black; heavy body; short legs; thickly covered with long, sharp, quills; deep red eyeshine; 18 to 22 inches long; 7- to-9-inch tail; 10 to 28 pounds.

Similar species: none.

Habitat/Distribution: Forested areas throughout the region and in RMNP.

Food: Summer—leaves, seeds, and buds of shrubs; grasses and forbs. Winter—buds, twigs, and inner bark of trees—especially aspen and ponderosa pine.

Armed as it is with between 15,000 and 30,000 needle-sharp quills, this slow-moving rodent is as impervious to attack as the skunk. The quills, equipped with barbs that flair out from the shaft when imbedded in warm, moist flesh, not only resist being pulled out but also readily work themselves in. Spread out along the back and sides from the forehead to the tip of the tail, these quills deter many would-be predators.

When challenged, the porcupine simply puts its head between its forelegs and turns its rump to the enemy. If touched anywhere, the porcupine slaps at the intruder with its muscular tail. If contact is made, the quills are driven deep into the attacker, who will probably give up immediately. However, some predators, notably the cougar and the fisher, have learned to slide a paw underneath the porcupine, flip it on its back, and attack its soft belly. Even this method is not foolproof, as researchers in some areas have found that a majority of cougars have porcupine quills imbedded in their forelimbs.

The porcupine is primarily nocturnal but may be seen resting in treetops during the day. It does not climb well but is more comfortable in trees than on the ground. It is solitary in the summer but more gregarious in winter.

Dens are located in a hollow log or a natural cave. The single kit is born in April or May after a seven-month gestation period. Weighing about a pound at birth, it has its eyes open and comes equipped with a complete set of quills that harden within hours after birth.

Porcupines love salt and they love to chew. As a result, they often damage trees, buildings, communication lines, radiator hoses, and wooden hand tools such as axe handles.

Porcupine —T. J. Ulrich

Porcupine chewing on antler —T. J. Ulrich

Porcupine damage —J. L. Wassink

Order Lagomorpha
Rabbits, Hares, and Pikas

Rabbits, hares, and pikas make up the order Lagomorpha. These mammals are distinctive in that they have two pairs of upper incisors that they use to clip off the plant material they live on. Chewing is done with a transverse movement rather than the rotary motion used by the rodents. Lagomorphs have short tails and long hind legs.

Members of this order have an interesting habit called "coprophagy." Soft, glutinous pellets are secreted in the evening or early morning and are immediately reingested. Digesting this material twice allows these mammals to assimilate certain vitamins that would otherwise be lost. Pellets voided at other times are hard and dry and are not reingested.

Pikas belong to the family **Ochotonidae.** Active from dawn to about 11 A.M., the pika has a scurrying gait resembling that of a mouse. Pikas live in colonies and have three or four young per year, which are born naked and helpless. They are small, have small, rounded ears, and no visible tail.

The family **Leporidae** includes the rabbits and hares. They have long ears, long hind legs, and a short tail. They move by hopping, and move about primarily under cover of darkness. Usually solitary, the members of this family are very prolific and may raise several litters of up to eight young per year. Populations of rabbits and hares may fluctuate wildly in relation to weather and forage conditions.

Pika —J. L. Wassink

Snowshoe hare —J. L. Wassink

Cottontail rabbit sunbathing —J. L. Wassink

Pika

Description: Short, dense, gray-brown fur; roundish body; short legs; large head with short, round ears; no visible tail; 8 inches long, about 4 ounces.

Similar species: none.

Habitat/Distribution: Rocky fields in alpine and subapline meadows throughout the region and in RMNP.

Food: Most vegetation—grasses, sedges, forbs.

Huddled motionless on a rock, the pika is difficult to spot. Consequently, hikers usually hear the pika before seeing it. The ventriloquist qualities of its call mask the source of the sound. Uttered at the first sign of danger, the call is picked up by nearby pikas and echoed throughout the colony. If danger comes too close, the little animal disappears beneath an overhanging rock or through a small chink in the rocks.

In fall, pikas begin building "haystacks." They leave the security of their rock piles and follow well-worn paths to nearby grassy meadows. There they clip off bits of vegetation with their sharp front teeth. These are carried back to rock piles and spread out to cure in the sun. The piles grow slowly, as lichens, grasses, blossoming herbs, Oregon grape, lungwort, huckleberry, raspberry, cranberry, serviceberry, sagebrush, snowberry, thistles, nettles, twigs, leaves, and pine needles are added to the cache. Eventually, each pika may have three or four bushel-sized haystacks. If rain threatens before the stacks are cured, the pika scurries to carry its harvest, one mouthful at a time, to the shelter of a rocky burrow. Once cured, the materials are stored in the rocky labyrinths where the pika makes its home.

Throughout the bitter cold and piercing winds of the frigid alpine winters, the pika stays warm and dry beneath the sheltering blanket of snow—sustained by its stores of "hay."

Spring brings the breeding season. Born anytime from late May to early September, the young are born naked and helpless. Able to walk in a week and fully mature in six weeks, young pikas must establish a territory and stockpile their winter food supply before the snows come again. Young born too late to accomplish these tasks before winter do not survive until spring.

Pika —W. Shattil & R. Rozinski

Pika —J. L. Wassink

Pika haystack —J. L. Wassink

Rabbits are separated from the hares by their proportionately shorter ears and hind legs. Their young are born blind, naked, and helpless, with their eyes tightly closed, in a carefully constructed nest. Cottontails are one of the most abundant mammals in the nation. A favorite target of hunters in the East, they have been widely studied for decades.

Eastern Cottontail *Sylvilagus floridanus*

Description: Brownish on back with tan on lower back and rump; cinnamon on sides extends down to white underparts; outside of ears are darker than back and whitish inside; white powderpuff tail; 14 to 17 inches long; 2 to 4 pounds.

Similar species: Nuttall's cottontail—smaller size; lighter color; shorter ears. Desert cottontail—smaller in size; lighter color; longer ears. Jackrabbits and snowshoe hare—much larger.

Habitat/Distribution: Brushy areas, weed patches, and other areas with varied vegetation where soil is rich. Found in foothills along eastern edge of region, not found in RMNP.

Food: Summer—tender herbaceous plants; Winter—twigs and bark of young trees.

Active most of the night, cottontails spend their days resting in a small depression, called a "form," hidden in tall grass, in thick brush, or beneath a brush pile. Young are born anytime from March to September in a slight depression in the ground hidden by grasses. Adults may have three or four litters per year in good habitat.

Nuttall's or Mountain Cottontail *Sylvilagus nuttallii*

Description: Grizzled yellowish gray above; whitish below; tail is black above and white below; ears edged with white or buffy inside, black outside; 14 to 17 inches long; 1½ to 3 pounds.

Similar species: Eastern cottontail—larger; darker; longer ears. Desert cottontail—lighter color; longer ears. Jackrabbits and snowshoe hare—much larger.

Habitat/Distribution: Borders between forest and plain, brush lands, rocky outcroppings, thick sagebrush, and shrubby areas near agricultural land throughout the region and in RMNP.

Food: Summer—tender herbaceous plants; Winter—twigs and bark of young trees.

Cottontails may spend their entire life on a single acre. They spend their days lying in forms and dusting, and their nights feeding. Camouflage is their first line of defense, but they are never more than a couple of quick bounds from nearby cover.

Eastern cottontail —J. L. Wassink

Nuttall's cottontail —J. L. Wassink
Desert cottontail —J. L. Wassink

Hares and Jackrabbits have longer ears and hind legs than the rabbits. The young are born in the open, fully furred and with their eyes wide open, and are able to run about within hours after birth.

Snowshoe Hare *Lepus americanus*

Description: Summer—reddish brown or brownish above, whitish or buffy below; disproportionately large feet; ears relatively short, brownish with black on the back. Winter—white overall except the tips of the ears; 12 to 18 inches; 2 to 4 pounds.

Similar species: Black-tailed jackrabbit—long ears, black stripe down rump and on top of tail. White-tailed jackrabbit—long ears, larger size.

Habitat/Distribution: Found in brush patches in coniferous forests and swampy areas in higher elevations throughout the region and in RMNP.

Food: Vegetation—mostly buds, twigs, and bark of woody plants, such as red and white pine, white spruce, birch, aspen, and willow; tender herbaceous plants in summer.

The snowshoe hare is also known as the varying hare because its color varies with the seasons. With the coming of winter, the snowshoe hare develops dense hair pads between its toes. These pads, coupled with oversized feet, act like snowshoes, giving the animal mobility in deep snow and its common name. The principal food of the lynx and also frequently taken by fox, fisher, marten, hawks, and owls, snowshoes rarely live more than three years in the wild.

Because they are found in brushy thickets of the coniferous forests and are nocturnal, they are seldom seen except along roadsides. More sociable than the other hares, several snowshoes may be found in close proximity to each other. They occupy a home range of about 10 to 15 acres. They maintain runways through the thick brush, which maximize their chances of escaping from their many enemies.

Courtship involves thumping the ground with the hind feet. As the excitement escalates, the courting hares chase each other in a series of circles, sometimes even somersaulting over each other. They do not nest, but give birth in a slight depression that the precocious young soon abandon.

Small clearings, creating brushy cover and more browse, can increase the number of hares. When abundant, snowshoe hares can cause a lot of damage to young trees by debarking them.

Snowshoe hare, summer pelage —T. J. Ulrich

Snowshoe hare, fall coat —T. J. Ulrich

Snowshoe hare, winter coat —J. L. Wassink

Young snowshoe hare —T. J. Ulrich

Black-tailed Jackrabbit   *Lepus californicus*

Description: Grayish brown above, grizzled with black, and buffy white below; long ears tipped with black; tail—black above, buffy gray below; 16 to 21 inches long; 3 to 7 pounds.

Similar species: Snowshoe hare—small ears, small size, white tail. White-tailed jackrabbit—white tail.

Habitat/Distribution: Found in sagebrush, lower foothill grasslands, and adjacent hayfields throughout the lower elevations of the region and in RMNP.

Food: Vegetarian—shrubs, grasses, and weedy plants.

A sensitive nose, eyes set far back on their heads, and huge ears that can detect the muted sound of a coyote as its fur brushes lightly against the grass, black-tailed jackrabbits are equipped for survival. When threatened, they first freeze, laying their ears over their backs and blending their long, lean bodies into the surroundings. If the vanishing act fails, powerful legs carry them to safety. Capable of running at speeds up to 35 miles per hour, leaping 6 feet high or 20 feet forward and changing directions with every leap, they are not easy to catch. Still, they fall prey to a wide variety of avian and mammalian predators.

White-tailed Jackrabbit   *Lepus townsendii*

Description: Large hare; summer—grayish above and white below with primarily white tail; winter—white or whitish overall except for dark ear tips; 18 to 22 inches long; 5 to 10 pounds.

Similar species: Snowshoe hare—small size, small ears. Black-tailed jackrabbit—black stripe down rump and on top of tail.

Habitat/Distribution: Found in grasslands and higher grassy sagebrush of the foothills and mountains throughout the region and in RMNP.

Food: Vegetarian—shrubs, grasses, and weedy plants.

The white-tailed jackrabbit seems to be giving way to the invasion of black-tailed jackrabbits. Their white coloration in winter provides excellent camouflage in snow, but makes them easy targets in snow-free winters, when they fall prey to predators. The most serious threat to the white-tail seems to be the loss of bunchgrass through alteration of the habitat by over-use and conversion to other forms of agriculture.

Black-tailed jackrabbit —B. Gerlach/Visuals Unlimited

White-tailed jackrabbit —T. J. Ulrich

White-tailed jackrabbit, winter coat —J. L. Wassink

Order Chiroptera
Bats

The order **Chiroptera** (meaning "hand-wing") includes the bats, the only true flying mammals. Elongated fingers, joined by a membrane that extends to the hind legs and on to the tail, give them aerial abilities equal to those of birds.

Although they are nocturnal, bats do not have exceptional night vision. Instead, they navigate and hunt by echo-location. When flying, they emit 50 to 60 high-pitched cries per second that range in frequency from 30,000 cycles per second (the upper limit of human hearing) to 75,000 cycles or higher. The bat can tell from the echo pattern whether it is coming from an obstacle or potential food, and it can read the pattern to determine direction and distance to the interception point. Their echo-location is precise enough to locate and capture flying insects or slip through obstacles as formidable as a maze of closely strung wires. Precise enough, in fact, to capture an average of 3,000 gnats, flies, and mosquitoes each night.

Bats in the Central Rockies eat mainly insects. They have huge appetites and must eat more than half their weight every night because of their extremely high metabolic rate. Their heart rates, about 700 beats per minute, are outdone only by the shrews. Most animals with high metabolic rates are correspondingly short lived. However, bats are capable of going into torpor almost at will. If insects stop flying during a cold spell, bats can take a "snooze" until things warm up. Those species that don't fly south in winter seek out a sheltered cave and hibernate. As a result, bats may live to the ripe old age of twenty.

Perhaps the most maligned and misunderstood mammals in the Central Rockies, bats do not deserve their sinister reputations. They are not blind, nor vicious, their incidence of rabies is lower than that of many other animals, and they have no desire to fly into women's hair. They are intelligent, clean, gentle, and the best insect zappers around.

Little brown myotis —J. L. Wassink

Family Vespertilionidae

The family **Vespertilionidae** are the plainnose bats. They have unmodified noses, complete interfemoral membranes, and tails that do not extend beyond the back edge of the membrane.

Little Brown Myotis   *Myotis lucifugus*

Description: Yellowish-brown upper parts and light buff underparts; wing membrane extends between the hind legs and the tail; feet are blackish brown; ears, when laid forward, do not extend beyond the nose.

Similar species: Many similar species but too similar to separate unless in hand.

Habitat/Distribution: Most common in forested areas throughout the region and in RMNP.

Food: Insects.

These bats forage along small rivers and streams or through cuts in the dense forest soon after sundown. Gregarious, they roost singly or in groups in caves, crevices in rocks or buildings, in hollow trees, or under bark slabs. A single offspring is born each year, which may cling to the mother until it gets large enough to hinder the mother during flight. It then stays at the roost site while the female is foraging until it is capable of hunting for itself.

Little brown myotis —J. L. Wassink

Order Insectivora
Insectivores

The order **Insectivora** consists of the moles and shrews. As their name implies, they eat mostly insects. They are believed to be rather primitive, have weak eyes, walk plantigrade, and have five toes on each foot.

Family Soricidae

Shrews (family **Soricidae**), the smallest mammals in the region, are widespread. They have the highest metabolic rate of any of the mammals and must eat almost constantly. Because they burn energy at such a high rate, shrews must consume more than their body weight in food every day.

Driven by their enormous appetites, shrews are formidable predators and consume a variety of insects and invertebrates (earthworms, sow bugs, centipedes, spiders, slugs). Equipped with a poison gland in its mouth that secrets a potent nerve poison similar to that of some venomous snakes, shrews can and do prey on mice, which may outweigh them by five times. A mouse bitten by a shrew dies within minutes, but a human bitten by a shrew will merely experience discomfort.

Shrews build nests of dry grass or leaves in stumps, logs, or rock crevices. They have between two and nine young in a litter and may have more than one litter each year. The newborn open their eyes in about a week and they are weaned at about three weeks.

Most common in moist habitats, shrews are beneficial to have around because of the large number of insects they eat. Shrews, in turn, are eaten by snakes, weasels, foxes, and owls.

Identification of shrews is difficult, even if you are holding them in your hand. In addition, their ranges and habitats may overlap considerably. Skull characteristics are the only sure way of identifying them.

The **Vagrant Shrew** (*Sorex vagrans*) prefers damp areas such as marshes, wet meadows, ditch bottoms and sides, and fern jungles at medium to low elevations in the northern part of the region. The **Water Shrew** (*Sorex palustris*) lives near streams lush with vegetation and is one of the most interesting shrews. It might be seen scampering across water, a feat made possible by little bubbles of air trapped by the stiff hairs fringing its large feet. The **Montane Shrew** (*Sorex monticolus*) is also common in the Central Rockies.

Vagrant shrew —J. L. Wassink

Vagrant shrew showing pointed snoot —J. L. Wassink
Vagrant shrew portrait —J. L. Wassink

Order Marsupialia
Marsupials

The order **Marsupialia** is represented in North America by a single species, the opossum. Like all mammals, marsupials bear live young and nourish them by suckling. Marsupials lack a typical placenta, and their young are born in a very underdeveloped stage. The newborn young find their way to a special pouch where the mother's nipples are located, and continue to develop there. The lack of a typical placenta and their dentition are the characteristics that separate them from other mammals. Marsupials also have small brains, short legs, five toes, and long tails.

Virginia Opossum

Family Didelphidae

Didelphis virginiana

Description: Gray or blackish gray fur; long, pointed snout; black ears; short legs; heavy body; long, naked, scaly prehensile tail. Males, 15 to 21 inches long; 8-to-20-inch tail; 6 to 14 pounds. Females, slightly smaller, 4 to 8 pounds.

Habitat/Distribution: Found in deciduous growth along streams. Opossums are relatively rare in the region and are not found in RMNP.

Food: Omnivorous—nuts, fruits, vegetables, eggs, meat, and carrion.

The only marsupial found in the continental United States, the opossum is almost exclusively nocturnal. When seen in headlights, they have a dull orange eyeshine. By day, opossums stay hidden in a hollow tree or log, a rock cave, or an earth den scratched out by another mammal.

A single litter of up to eighteen young is born after a gestation of twelve days. The size of a honeybee and weighing about one-fifth of an ounce when born, the blind, naked young somehow find their way to the mother's pouch. There, they attach themselves to a teat, where they remain for the next 50 to 65 days. After detaching themselves, they venture out of the pouch and may be seen riding on their mother's back.

When disturbed, the opossum will disappear into the first hole or crevice it can find. When cornered, the opossum at first bares its teeth. If that fails to sidetrack the attacker, an occasional opossum, perhaps one in ten, may feign death by falling on its side, closing its eyes, and extending its tongue.

The opposable big toe on the hind foot and the prehensile tail, which can grasp almost as well as a hand, aid opossums in climbing. The tail is also used extensively in carrying things, such as nesting materials to the den.

The main factor preventing opossums from extending their range to the north and to higher elevations is cold temperatures.

Virginia opossum —T. J. Ulrich

Virginia opossums threatening —T. J. Ulrich

Virginia opossum portrait —T. J. Ulrich

Virginia opossum showing prehensile tail
—T. J. Ulrich

Glossary

Alpine—inhabiting or growing in the mountains above timberline.

Antlers—bony growths that occur on the heads of the deer family.

Browse—to feed on the twigs and leaves of woody plants.

Carnivore—an animal that feeds primarily on the flesh of other animals.

Carrion—the decaying flesh of dead animals.

Coniferous—cone-bearing plants.

Coprophagy—practice of consuming their own feces, as do rabbits and some rodents.

Crepuscular—appearing or active at dawn and dusk.

Cud—a ball of food forced up into the mouth from the first stomach of a ruminant and chewed over again.

Deciduous—plants that drop their leaves every year.

Delayed implantation—a phenomenon in which the fertilized egg, ovum, develops to the blastocyst stage and then lies dormant in the uterus until suitable day length results in proper conditions for development.

Digitigrade—walks on the toes without using the sole of the foot.

Diurnal—active during the daylight hours.

Foliage—leaves of a tree or bush.

Forbs—herbaceous plants other than grasses.

Graze—to feed primarily on grasses and forbs.

Gregarious—tendency to live or move in groups.

Herbivore—animal that feeds primarily on plant material—stems, leaves, and seeds.

Hibernation—to pass the winter in a dormant state.

Horns—bony growths on the heads of goats, sheep, bison, and cattle.

Incisors—front teeth adapted for cutting or gnawing.

Induced ovulation—the release of an egg from the ovary requires outside stimulation of some kind.

Keratin—a compound that forms the essential ingredient in horny tissues like horns, hooves, and claws.

Larvae—immature young of insects and invertebrates.

Molars—broad, flat teeth located behind the canine teeth, used for grinding.

Monogamous—a species that breeds with only one individual during a breeding cycle.

Montane—pertaining to, growing in, or inhabiting mountainous regions; the lower vegetation belt on mountains.

Nocturnal—active at night.

Nomadic—wandering from place to place, seemingly without a pattern.

Omnivorous—an organism that eats both vegetable and animal matter.

Parturition—the act of giving birth.

Pedicel—a bony protrusion that rises from the frontal bone and forms the base of antlers.

Pelage—the hair or fur covering a mammal.

Photoperiod—the interval in a 24-hour day when an animal is exposed to light.

Plantigrade—walking on the soles of the feet.

Polygamous—a species that breeds with more than one mate during a single breeding cycle.

Prehensile—capable of precise movement and adapted for grasping or holding by wrapping around.

Prolific—able to produce large numbers of offspring.

Ruminant—even-toed, cud-chewing mammals such as deer, sheep, and cattle, which have four-chambered stomachs.

Rump—the back portion of a mammal surrounding the tail.

Rut—a period of sexual excitement; the breeding season of large ungulates.

Scavenger—a mammal that feeds on carrion, garbage, or the leftovers of other animal's kills.

Solitary—a mammal that prefers to live alone and avoids the company of others of its species.

Species—a group of animals exhibiting common characteristics that interbreed and produce fertile young when given the opportunity.

Territory—a section of habitat that an individual, breeding pair, or other group actively defend against others of the same species.

Testosterone—a male sex hormone.

Torpor—a state in which the metabolism drops to abnormally low levels; a means of conserving energy.

Ungulate—one of the hoofed mammals.

Suggested References

Mammal Identification and Biology

Burt, William Henry. *A Field Guide to the Mammals*. Houghton Mifflin Company, Boston, 1964. 284 pp.

Burton, John A. *Mammals*. Smithmark Publishers, New York, 1991. 192 pp.

Burton, Maurice. *The New Larouse Encyclopedia of Animal Life*. Bonanza Books, New York, 1980. 640 pp.

Burton, Maurice, and Robert Burton. *Inside the Animal World—An encyclopedia of animal behavior*. Quadrangle/The New York Times Book Co., 1977. 316 pp.

Davis, David E., and Frank B. Golley. *Principles in Mammalogy*. Van Nostrand Reinhold Company, New York, 1965. 335 pp.

Halfpenny, James. *A Field Guide to Mammal Tracking in North America*. Johnson Publishing Company, Boulder, Colorado, 1986. 164 pp.

National Wildlife Federation. "Gardening with Wildlife Kit." National Wildlife Federation, 1412 Sixteenth Street N.W., Washington, D.C. 20036.

Novak, Milan, et al. *Wild Furbearer Management and Conservation in North America*. Ontario Ministry of Natural Resources, Toronto, 1987. 1,150 pp.

Rennicke, Jeff. *Colorado Wildlife*. Falcon Press, Helena, Montana, 1990. 138 pp.

Rue III, Leonard Lee. *Furbearing Animals of North America*. Crown Publishers, Inc., New York, 1981. 343 pp.

Taylor, Walter P., et al. *The Deer of North America*. The Wildlife Management Institute and Stackpole Company, Harrisburg, Pennsylvania, 1969. 669 pp.

Wernert, Susan J. *North American Wildlife.* Reader's Digest Association, Inc., New York, 1982. 576 pp.

Locating and Observing Mammals

Bat Conservation International, Inc. c/o Brackenridge Field Laboratory. University of Texas. Austin, Texas 78712

Bissel, Steven J., et al. *Colorado Mammal Distribution Latilong Study.* Colorado Division of Wildlife, 1982. 25 pp.

Brainerd, John W. *The Nature Observer's Handbook.* The Globe Pequot Press, Chester, Connecticut, 1986. 255 pp.

Brown, Vinson. *Reading the Woods.* Stackpole Books, Harrisburg, Pennsylvania, 1969. 159 pp.

Carpenter, Leslie Benjamin. *Idaho Wildlife Viewing Guide.* Falcon Press, Helena, Montana, 1990. 104 pp.

Cole, Jim. *Utah Wildlife Viewing Guide.* Falcon Press, Helena, Montana, 1990. 88 pp.

Gray, Mary Taylor. *Colorado Wildlife Viewing Guide.* Falcon Press, Helena, Montana, 1992. 128 pp.

Halfpenny, James. *A Field Guide to Mammal Tracking in North America.* Johnson Publishing Company, Boulder, Colorado, 1986. 164 pp.

Hanenkrat, Frank T. *Wildlife Watcher's Handbook.* Winchester Press, New York, 1977. 241 pp.

Lechleitner, R. R. *Wild Mammals of Colorado.* Pruett Publishing Company, Boulder, Colorado, 1969. 254 pp.

National Wildlife Federation Books. *America's Wildlife Hideaways.* Washington, D.C., 1989. 239 pp.

Riley, Laura, and William Riley. *Guide to the National Wildlife Refuges.* Anchor Press/Doubleday, Garden City, New York, 1979. 653 pp.

Seton, Ernest Thompson. *Animal Tracks and Hunter Signs.* Doubleday & Company, Inc., Garden City, New York, 1958. 160 pp.

Index

—D. M. Wassink

Jan Wassink studied wildlife management at Colorado State University and Utah State University and has photographed wildlife for over twenty years. He wrote and photographed *Birds of the Central Rockies*, a companion to this volume published by Mountain Press, and *Idaho Wildlife*, in the American Geographic series. His credits include articles and photographs in *National Wildlife, Natural History, Ranger Rick, Living Bird Quarterly, Fur, Fish & Game, BBC Wildlife, Utah Outdoors,* and *Montana Magazine*.

Wassink lives in Kalispell, Montana, with his wife and three sons.